CREATING
RELATIONSHIP
WELLNESS

CREATING RELATIONSHIP WELLNESS

An Introduction to the Techniques of Mindfulness for Healthy Relationships

Stephanie Wijkstrom, LPC

Universal-Publishers
Irvine • Boca Raton

Creating Relationship Wellness:
An Introduction to the Techniques of Mindfulness for Healthy Relationships

Universal Publishers, Inc.
Irvine • Boca Raton
USA • 2021
www.Universal-Publishers.com

ISBN: 978-1-62734-337-4 (pbk.)
ISBN: 978-1-62734-338-1 (ebk.)

Typeset by Medlar Publishing Solutions Pvt Ltd, India
Cover design by Ivan Popov

Library of Congress Cataloging-in-Publication Data

Names: Wijkstrom, Stephanie, 1982- author.
Title: Creating relationship wellness : an introduction to the techniques of mindfulness for healthy relationships / Stephanie Wijkstrom.
Description: Irvine : Universal Publishers, 2021. | Includes bibliographical references.
Identifiers: LCCN 2021006463 (print) | LCCN 2021006464 (ebook) | ISBN 9781627343374 (paperback) | ISBN 9781627343381 (ebook)
Subjects: LCSH: Man-woman relationships. | Couples--Psychology. | Interpersonal relations. | Mindfulness (Psychology)
Classification: LCC HQ801 .W6956 2021 (print) | LCC HQ801 (ebook) | DDC 306.7--dc23
LC record available at https://lccn.loc.gov/2021006463
LC ebook record available at https://lccn.loc.gov/2021006464

DEDICATION

To my husband Martin Wijkstrom, the greatest joy that I have known is loving you. I hope I tell you in ways that you can feel and understand, that you are my greatest inspiration. Even if there were a way to have a hundred lifetimes together, there could never be enough time for me to cherish your smile, your brilliantly curious mind, and your wise and patient heart.

TABLE OF CONTENTS

CHAPTER ONE

A GUIDE TO NAVIGATING THIS BOOK

Understanding mindfulness is the means to creating relationship wellness, but most of us need guidance to be capable of nourishing love with our conscious awareness. We know that few things touch us as deeply as when we are falling in love, but few things destroy us more thoroughly than losing our connection to that person we love. As humans, we live, we learn, we love, and in some ways, our love is the greatest legacy that we can leave on this earth during our limited time here. Perhaps you are finding this book in an frenzied effort to reclaim your stake on the feelings that once coursed within your relationship; perhaps you or your partner are thinking of ending things and you have agreed to one last ditch effort to whisk you both back to love. If the latter, I cannot help you. There is no recipe for resurrecting a dead relationship; rather, relationships must be allowed to die to then be reborn together in a different shape, formed anew with well-learned lessons and the optimism and curiosity that accompanies uncharted waters.

Let me introduce myself. I have spent 10 years practicing as a licensed counselor who specializes in helping people enhance their relationships. I am the founder of a large counseling center, and a significant part of what our center does is help people with their relationships, whether they are seeking premarital counseling, family counseling, or couples therapy. I have also come by the knowledge and skills I will share in this book through the trials and tribulations of being a woman who has loved, a woman who has loved terribly, and a woman who has loved in the action of every fiber of her being. In the span of my own life, I am very happily married to my husband. Each day together, we come together and love each other up. We nourish this marriage with our collective wisdom and desire to enjoy each moment together. We are also committed to fighting fairly, to maintaining our health and pursuing our professional interests outside of our love. Thus, we are whole when we connect as well as the ways in which we are separate. We both have taken much from our unique past experiences. Personally, in the two engagements and one marriage before this one, I floundered, made terrible decisions, allowed myself to be treated tragically, and felt full-fledged hatred in one especially troubling relationship.

Yet, the heart and desire to love prevails. When our mindset is focused on gaining understanding, even the hardest lessons become victories for our own human evolution. As a counselor, I do encounter this everyday. Couples enter therapy hoping to find a therapist to solve their problems; instead, good counseling is teaching couples how they can become their own agent of change to work towards solving their relationship issues. I help lovers look at things differently so they can respond differently. When they come to understand the core needs under their common disputes, they are called toward compassion, empathy, and connection. For example, when a couple has a particular disagreement about the laundry, I seek to understand what is happening in that disagreement, what the issue means to both of them and how they should go about solving their problems and getting their needs met in love.

If you show me a bitter person, I will show you a person who has lost much in love. If you show to me a joyous person, I will unveil to you a person who has lost much in love. The difference between them, and therein lies the art of remaining happy in romance, is that one deals with the loss and hurt very differently. They choose to focus intently on two aspects: first, on the spectrum of human experience, which means accepting losses and hurt as an important part of living in love, and then secondly, just as intently on gratitude, so that the hurt fades to the distance. It is a powerful exercise when I ask a couple to look at their partner and to share something that they are grateful for in them. Sometimes we hold on so tightly to our bitterness, and focus so much on the shortcomings of our love, that we forget to remember all that can be loved in them. Typically, when couples do the gratitude exercise, a cascade of tears erupt and a sort of tenderness emerges that fills both people in the room. What might happen to our love if we trained ourselves to focus on gratitude for our partner for at least a couple of minutes everyday?

If you are thinking this may be all quite jolly in theory, but can't imagine how this can apply to you, that is ok. I promise to illustrate to you within this text the ways that our mindset and response makes all the difference in our relationship outcomes. I have personally coached couples through tragedies like death, infidelity, and decades of sexlessness and disconnection. They have entered marriage counseling ready to walk the plank and end their commitments, but something held them back and they decided to try counseling instead. The collaboration of marriage counseling and their efforts worked. Through child care and work responsibilities, through years of hopelessness and fear, they succeed in creating a joyful, passionate, intimate marriage, and later, they were able to look back together and uncover the significance that those hardships had in shaping the strength of their newly built connection.

Love is eternal, connection a skill, yet, according to the National bureau of labor statistics, as many as 40% of marriages will end in divorce. By using the model of wellness and the path of mindfulness, we are called to understand what changes can be made to prevent relationships from suffering or declining. I have worked with thousands of couples, and I promise you this: all conflicted relationships walk the same foot path to demise and they enact the same destructive patterns, but they are each helpless to stop without learning a better way of managing their issues. Many tragedies of marital demise could be prevented by turning towards preventative methods that enrich our relationships, by utilizing the nurturing effects of consistent tenderness, by making the effort to reach understanding of each other, by working toward regular interplays that create shared meaning, by reaping the benefits of creating trust, and by collaborating to share mutual attention. Our goal in creating a mindful marriage is not only to have a relationship which stands the test of time, but more importantly, a blissful relationship brimming with loving wellness that is a well-adjusted and nourishing bond for both partners and the entire family.

Mindfulness is a mental state achieved by practicing non-judgmental, focused awareness on the thoughts, feelings, and bodily sensations which are evoked from observing the present moment. Sounds elegantly simple, right? The truth is, it is simple. Mindfulness truly is our natural state, the emotional and psychological current which courses through us when we unclutter our thoughts and unruffle our way of being. It is a natural reflex toward our innate state that allows us to achieve our optimal potential.

The only moment that we have is this one; we cannot go back to the early days, nor should we lapse into fretting over tomorrow. I assure you that those who encounter a marriage hoping to remain in the state of passion and the unknown, (the hallmark the earliest days of love), will forever miss the meaning of marriage. By living in the great expanse of now, we become mindful. When your partner arrives home from walking the dog, can you see them as they are, or are you still so angry over their non-response to yesterday's text that you fail to connect in this moment? Are you so worried that some doom may befall your bond next year that you don't even hear the door open, signaling their arrival? If you listen for the door, if you observe and pause to share a simple gratitude for walking the dog when they walk through the door, how might that feel in your own physical body? How might that feel for them? In this book, we will apply the core philosophy of mindfulness to enhance relationships—whether a marriage, long term dating partnership, or any other form of coupledom. We embrace mindfulness as the path to self-development.

What began in new-age spiritual communities has now turned into a hotbed of scientific inquiry, leading to the widely noted understanding that mindfulness aids us in accelerating our trajectory towards physical, emotional, and spiritual health. In a 2007 study by Barnes et al, it was found that mindfulness greatly affects our happiness in intimate relationships. According to the research, lovers report feeling more happiness in partnerships where mindfulness is practiced. Perhaps you are wondering how that works, how one's own psychological mindset can influence what happens in the world and in our relationship with others. While mindfulness for spiritual and psychological growth holds its merit, any practice becomes most relevant when it seeps into our interactions with the greater world. People who practice mindfulness exhibit a greater ability to regulate stress and emotions, as well as being significantly better at deescalating conflict than those couples who do not practice mindfulness. As this book will explicate, if you are going to have a shred of peace in a marriage, you must become very skilled at turning away from heated conflict and practicing forgiveness.

With so much to be gained by enhancing our mindfulness, this text devotes itself to helping the reader understand what exactly it means to practice it in the main areas of our love relationship, and how to achieve this beautiful state. Additionally, each chapter offers skill building exercises that we can strategically and consistently apply to enhance mindfulness techniques and utilize the scientifically validated and historically celebrated methodology of mindfulness. These exercises have been tested in the arena of my own marriage counseling practice and brought great results. The mechanisms of conscious awareness or mindfulness constitute a simple and accessible system of enhancement. Mindfulness is prized for its practicality and austere elegance by many around the globe. Its reach includes everyone from great spiritual leaders to business tycoons, as well as those on the path toward self-development. Everyone is able to apply this wisdom to enhance loving relationships.

To be mindful means that we practice focused awareness of our thoughts and actions by manifesting intimate consciousness of all of the vital parts of our being. The second component of the process is that we are non-judgmental. It is not enough to notice that we lapse into despair when a loved person is out of reach for a couple of hours at work; we should also not judge ourselves too harshly for this abandonment insecurity and instead find ways to adjust our attitude so that we don't respond to them with unconscious irritation when they reemerge. Just as when we practice any form of meditation, to be mindful, we first attune to our thoughts and feelings. When aiming the well-honed laser beam of our awareness towards ourselves, we simultaneously commit to suspending judgment about the contents of our cognitive and emotive terrain. Thus, all forms of compassion begin with the self.

We are not going to admire all of the contents of our consciousness, and we are not going to admire all of the things that our partner says or does on a daily basis. There will be some defensiveness, aggression, fear, lingering hurt, and maladaptive communication floating around in our minds and hearts. However, the benefits of adjusting our approach to relating are plenty. When we tune in, we will be better able to increase empathy and compassion for our beloved. This will forge a love that is inextricably woven within the deepest layers of consciousness, where we are attuned to the thoughts and feelings that our partner is immanently expressing. Like all things, mindfulness in our relationship with our partner or spouse is something that has to be continually practiced within a relationship, and one that must continually evolve depending upon where our relationship is in the moment. Just as in the rest of the relationship, collaboration will pair well with the efforts of this text. Relationship change will have the best outcome when two lovers are working toward becoming more mindful together.

There is much at stake here. The great Zen spiritual guru, Thich Nhat Hanh proffers the wisdom that "To love without knowing how to love, wounds the person we love." In my clinical and personal experience, it is evident that it takes great effort to learn how to sustain and enrich another person with our love. Let us not mistake the length of a relationship for the strength of its bond either. There are many people who stride through a mediocre twenty years of marriage feeling completely disconnected and only mildly unhappy, yet afraid to speak up. There are engagements that remain in their toxicity for many years, but they hold no strong bond of love. For any relationship that is suffering, you will find a couple that lacks the skills of understanding and connecting; yet the tools of mindfulness are within their reach. These tools represent a specific set of skills to help them improve the quality of their intimate interactions. Instead, they silently and bitterly lapse into the mires of discontent while their once cherished marriage slides down the cliff of unhappiness, leaving their shared daily life unbearable.

This book is for each lover in the world, to become mindful of the opportunities alive in the glorious and simple moments of each day. We will open ourselves to the opportunities that can be created as we are compelled toward the actions of mindful connection. These are ways to deepen our bonds and give us the tools to become mindful of ourselves and our partner, mindful of communication, mindful of intimacy, mindful of how we are connecting and ways to nurture that connection. Every rose bush will grow, but to continue producing roses, we must feed it, we must prune it, year after year after year. Yet isn't the scent and vibrancy of the rose's petals in full bloom worth the cost of the effort that went into tending it? Mindful relationships are a part of total body, mind, and spiritual wellness. We become well by recognizing the interplay between ourselves and each part of our being. Wellness allows us to outline and utilize preventative strategies and interventions which strengthen us and our relationships before they have the chance to fall into disrepair. The path to self and to loving relationship development is one to be walked with our head held high and faith in the eternal commitment of truly nourished love.

Each chapter of this text can be read together as a couple. Devoting one week to reading a chapter and completing its exercises will allow time for the kernels of understanding to be planted and for the skills to develop slowly in realistic and manageable chunks of time. Remember, long lasting change is a slow process, it is incremental, and skills build upon themselves in stages, so no quick or magical fixes here.

This book is intended to unfold exactly in this way, slowly as the intake of a long slow deep inhalation into our lungs. Others who are single or recovering from a divorce are also able to enjoy the teachings of this book. Perhaps you are recovering from a breakup and want to learn new tools to carry with you in your next effort to create lasting love. If that is the case, think about how different your last relationship was from the methods and process for loving that are discussed in these chapters. Use this as a new way of understanding yourself and any partner when you move forward in your life.

Here is a brief synopsis of the ideas discussed in each chapter:

1. **Curiously Me, Becoming Mindful of The Self:** Overview of thoughtful questions that will help the reader to gain a greater depth of understanding into their past, present, and to string together these concepts into an understanding of the self.

2. **Other, How Do I Know You My Dear Love?** In-depth considerations to transform the way that we think about who our partner is. Exercises to deepen your understanding of your partner. Questions to help you recreate the way you think about your partner, and to understand their sensitivities and personality on a different level.

3. **Merging, Two Whole Lovers Encounter Each Other and Create Harmony Together in a Mindful Marriage:** Looking at the points of contact, with emphasis on the two wholes of the individuals who are creating a healthy relationship. A battery of questions that will help you to assess the depth of closeness and understanding between you and your partner. This portion also takes into account some of the common points of conflict in troubled relationships.

4. **Communication, The Pathway to Communicating Mindfully:** A thorough examination of the many types of communication and communication styles, as well as their pitfalls. This will help the couple to experience a new way of experiencing their communication. This section will cue the reader into both

the giving and receiving end of communication, and ceaselessly encourages introspection and growth.

5. **Speaking Mindfully:** Not all words are the same. This will allow the reader to differentiate between the various layers of sharing with their partner. Along with each of the layers of communication, there are opportunities to understand how to take it deeper. This chapter ends with a week-long challenge meant to encourage long term change.

6. **From Emotional Reactivity to Mindfulness in Communication:** One major pitfall in relationships can happen when heightened emotions get in the way. This section is devoted to helping individuals and couples move beyond some of those common emotional hurdles. This includes practical exercises to modify behavior.

7. **Mindful Self-Care and Self-Soothing Strategies:** Self-care is always the cornerstone of every relationship. While it isn't always intuitive, we must care for ourselves to get anything else done. This section will help the reader to form a solid self-care plan. This is specifically in relation to emotionally reactive personality types.

8. **The Risk of Communication Avoidance and Inactivity.** This section examines the avoidant personality type in relationships and helps the person to overcome some of the potential hurdles to this style of relating.

9. **Mindful Make-Up: If You Want to Make Things Better, Listen Before You Speak:** While everyone knows how to have a disagreement, not everyone knows how to make it right afterwards. This will help each partner understand more about influencing their partner, and offers a step by step process for repairing after a disagreement.

10. **Being Accountable and Responsible:** This section is devoted to some internal mechanisms which will prevent discord from developing in a relationship, and addresses what will happen when we don't adopt these qualities.

11. **Forgiveness:** Some say that forgiveness is the alpha and omega of love. Here we enter a short discussion on what makes that so.

12. **Trust:** This section defines the different forms of trust that are necessary to foster a healthy relationship. After a thorough discussion into the important meanings of trust, the section provides some questions that that will serve as a trust building exercise.

13. **Creating a Relationship of Gratitude:** Gratitude is the currency of mindfulness. This section helps the reader to understand its mechanisms before finishing with some opportunities to deepen gratitude for one's own relationship and partner.

14. **Compassion and Empathy:** This section describes compassion and empathy within the relationship, and uncovers the ways that it can change over time within the marriage or couple.

15. **Patience:** Most people who are interested in mindfulness or meditation have learned many lessons about the importance of patience. This section will help you apply patience to your relationship.

16. **Creating an Emotionally Supportive Marriage or Relationship:** You aren't reading this because you want just any relationship— you want a good one! That means that you commit to giving and receiving emotional support. This section will define and help you create opportunities for this important function.

17. **Celebrating Joy:** Knowing how to connect with your partner over positive feelings and celebration is an important skill that will help to ensure the joy and longevity of your relationship.

18. **Intimacy:** Sexual intimacy is a celebration of a well-connected and mindful relationship. This section also includes an examination of potential barriers to intimacy, and it finishes with a full sensory battery of intimacy enhancing exercises.

19. **Mindfully Connecting Through Time:** This helps to form a road map for the passage of time, and shows how a mindful married or committed couple can continue to use time to deepen and enhance their bond.

20. **Conclusion.**

CHAPTER TWO

CURIOUSLY ME, BECOMING MINDFUL OF THE SELF

It all starts with the self and it is endlessly messy work. It is raw and painful when we are witnessing ourselves honestly. As they say, if we are going to get anything done in this world, we must begin with knowing ourselves. A component of that involves understanding our way of being in a relationship. Much like watching a good cinema production, we must know what major events have influenced our character development. We need to take a look at our emotional hygiene by coming to understand how we manage our emotions. Lastly, we need to create a method toward understanding and healing our childhood wounds.

Think, really intensely meditate upon this question: *Who are you?* Pause for a long time before responding. Put down this book and just be in your head for a bit while you think about this. When prompted to consider the answer to this, many people come up with responses that facilitate identification provided by their relationship to others, further illustrating the importance that we place on our relationships. For example, 'I am a wife and a mother.' Others may provide answers about their work, 'I am a Couples Therapist.' These answers, while they do identify parts of the self and what one does, they are not you! They do not completely grasp the ineffable components of being, all of the emotional, psychological, and even spiritual layers of the self that transcend job and relationships.

It often seems that it may be very easy to go along in life without developing true self-awareness, to plod along mindless of ourselves and of the deeper levels of our conscious awareness. Self-awareness means that we understand what our goals are, what brings us joy and sorrow, that we are keenly tuned into the phase of life that we are in, and have consciously created a set of values that serve as guidelines for our behavior. How do we process our feelings? In becoming mindful, it is not all about the fancy buzz words of gratitude and joy. We also must come to understand the shadow emotions, emotional realities like anger, jealousy, rigidity, demandingness. In the words of Carl Jung, "I would rather be whole than good." Becoming mindful and conscious of ourselves as we relate to our partner is a challenging goal. Think about your relationship and the way that you and your partner relate to each other. Just imagine your role in things. What If after you assess your total self you come to believe that you are perfect and everything that needs to be worked on in the relationship should be attributed to your partner? I can promise you, you have not been completely honest with yourself. The goal is to uncover which barriers exist within you that prevent the deeper love from unfolding.

Let us do some writing and reflecting to create a deeper awareness of ourselves. Remember that you don't need to show this to anyone so be very honest. Our current sense of self is influenced by our parental or caregiver relationships, as well as school year experiences, then work relationships, and even our self-perception. Let's look at those years and experiences, as well as current day concerns. Consider these questions:

> Were your basic childhood needs of food, shelter, and safety met?
>
> Who were the most important people in your life as a child and why?
>
> What made you feel safe and valued as a child?
>
> How did your parents or caregivers relate to each other?

What was their relationship like?

When you were upset, what did your caregivers do to soothe you?

What did you do to soothe yourself as a child?

What did you learn about emotions in your childhood?

How did your family talk about or manage feelings?

How did your family manage conflict?

How were you instructed and taught lessons as a kid?

What forms of punishment did your caregivers use?

What was your biggest challenge in childhood?

What were you most proud of as a child?

Who was the first person you loved?

What are five words that describe your style of being in a relationship now?

How do you communicate about problems with your partner?

What are some things that you would like to change about yourself?

What are the barriers to making those changes?

What brings you peace and hope now?

By doing a self-analysis and becoming unwaveringly introspective, we enter the pathway of demystifying the self. What were once mysterious and unconscious actions, the disagreements that hallmarked our past relationships instead become learning opportunities. The pathway towards understanding how the parts of our own character fit into our past and present will be a lifelong one. Remember the great Greek philosopher Socrates who said, "The unexamined life is not worth living." Mindfulness will aid us in plotting a trajectory for how our character can be developed. Think for a moment about the weeds of consciousness, the overgrowth beneath our shrubs which could be plucked away, preventing us from continually stumbling over the same roadblocks on our life path.

Relationship Understanding, one component of knowing the self is also knowing what is important to you in a relationship; so consider these things too. Are you reading this book all while imagining that the issues your relationship experiences should be fixed by your partner? What if I told you that is completely wrong, that instead, each of the perpetual issues in your relationship are clues into the unfolding of your own character and they represent areas that you can work on. What do you think is most important in a relationship? Does it include honesty, commitment, devotion, spiritual connection, monogamy, family, freedom, personal space? Probably all of those things or at least some of them are relevant to you in achieving awareness of your relationship values. How do you respond when you feel those issues are being violated or unsupported?

Imagine that freedom is placed high in your value system. While some may say it is difficult to have freedom in a relationship, I do not think that is true. We can be both merged and separate. What happens when your partner starts to inquire about the fifth round of golf you played this week? Do you explode, thinking how dare they ask about your time and freedom? The precipitating event and the response are always great places to analyze as they are often where our sources of miserable strife lie. Do you know what this situation represents to your partner, or are you so hyper-focused on your own needs that you fail to ask good questions that could lead you to see how the extended golf days violate your partner's core value of connection? Think about this very honestly.

Values are an integral part of the relationship. A person who holds no values can have no real relationship. A value system creates a way for lovers to prioritize actions. They also give us the chance to feel pride in our strengths and to develop our character. Without a value system, we are subject to chasing whatever shiny impulse presents itself around each corner. In contrast, by adhering to self-created values, we develop character, respect for ourselves and gain respect from others. Posit that we value commitment. We have practiced and enhanced our monogamous connection to our partner for years, and although at times we may notice others who are attractive or kind, we do not violate our commitment because that would shatter our values. This is an example of a value.

Time makes our relationship grow stronger

We all have different motivations for desiring the things that we hold passion for. We become mindful by examining the personal meanings attached to our decision to enter into a relationship with, and to remain committed to our partner or spouse. There are likely many reasons for the decision. Go ahead and ask yourself, why do you wake up each day still honoring your commitment? Some of us may become a little uncomfortable as we poke around in the layers of our unconscious and attempt to peel away at the layers of meaning embedded in our decision-making. Being committed to our relationships is a daily decision, although we don't always perceive it this way. If you don't recognize that, it's likely you feel trapped and suffocated. To be in love, we must actively choose to take part in being together every single day, and there will be times when we do not want to choose our marriage. We may want to work a few extra hours but our partner is waiting for us at home, and then we must choose between two competing scenarios. Some common reasons that we anchor ourselves into our commitment are that we care for our partner: we love them and we feel that they love us. We appreciate the time we spend together and we look forward to more time together. We love to parent together, we respect our lover, and we may even feel that we need our partner. It is likely that our daily decision to be in the relationship has something to do with our values, emotional, and physical needs being met.

It's essential to be aware of our deepest thoughts and impulses. The development of mindful self-awareness is not necessarily a comfortable process. The more these considerations feel slightly odd, the more we know we are doing something which deviates from our typical blind forward motion. When we feel a little uncomfortable, it may be a signal that we are outside of the comfort zone of our value system. Alternately, when reflecting upon our motivation to be a part of our relationship, we will gain confidence if we realize that we have taken the time to date, to experience love, then we will glitter with a perception which is strengthened by wisdom of past experience.

We have become very aware of ourselves and our needs. Thus, the character of the person we choose aligns with our own personality in such a way that the interactions of our daily life reaches the benchmark of our unique version of a good relationship. Awareness is a worthy goal.

Despite the importance of knowing ourselves and our motivations for being in a relationship, some people manage to enter and remain in a relationship for a long time without it. Others purposefully evade nurturing greater understanding. They sort of trod along in life. Maybe they are twenty years on in their marriage but feel unhappy about it because they don't believe that they have ever actively chosen anything in their whole lives. Imagine a woman who was told all of the time that she should get married as soon as she was old enough, and that she should look forward to having a grand and opulent wedding. Being a young woman who takes great pride in pleasing others, she was dutifully courted by a young man in her neighborhood and said yes when the proposal followed three months later. Although some people may end up developing themselves alongside their partner, feeling very happy in their marriage, others do not. Someone like this woman could spend considerable time wondering about that choice as the years go on. It may be difficult to remain within the relationship. The contract and decisions to commit were made very early in life, before ever really developing herself, and she may find herself always wondering what life may have been like if she had followed a passion or done something on her own. *What if I had gone to college or pursued my art for a few years before starting my family?*

There are many questions that we should ask ourselves. Part of knowing what we love and why means understanding the layers of fear and discontent. Life is in fact a journey. We will always be evolving in one direction or another. It takes awareness and finesse to grow internally as individuals as well as together with our partner.

Use this as a conversation point with your partner. Ask each other this: what parts of yourself do you feel that you are not being nurtured right now? What dreams or wishes are you harboring in secret? It's ok to say it even if it feels silly. When we become very aware of the values that inform our decision making, we are then capable of attuning this awareness to creating and sustaining the kind of relationship capable of nurturing ourselves and our beloved on an emotional, physical, and spiritual level.

Our internal development and personality begin to take root in childhood, and our capacity for understanding our partner is viewed through a certain lens of innate hope and fear until we reconcile our misgivings and develop our character. We should also become acquainted with our partner's values and motivations. When we hold those values to be sacred, we know to nurture those matters of vital importance to us and our beloved. We will work tirelessly to maintain the internal commitment to our values. Our ability to choose and adhere to any given path is a product of self-understanding, even self-discipline. We can more easily affirmatively choose our direction in life and feel confident about it the more we examine ourselves. Examining the self and developing character happens as we spend time taking risks, making glorious mistakes that form a mottled road map for our personal identity.

CHAPTER THREE

OTHER, HOW DO I KNOW YOU MY DEAR LOVE?

We hold their hand, but do we know their heart? I once heard an anonymous quote, "Love isn't about us, but it is about the other." When we commit to a relationship or marriage, we vow that we will offer our attention and presence in the service of moving closer to the inner being and life of our partner. It takes mindfulness and daily effort to understand our spouse. Some partners spend lots of time in the same room together, but hardly know each other, resulting in the hurt of mutual invisibility. Yet others can smilingly recite each delicate nuance about their partner, cradling shared memories as a treasure trove of love. They hold this knowledge like a badge of honor. I can tell you that right now, my husband's greatest enthusiasm outside of our marriage is working on his golf game. In the early days of falling in love, we talked in great detail about both of our pasts: I shared my truths, teen years of wild abandon and wandering like a nomad through Europe and South East Asia as an early adult. I uncloaked all of my vulnerable mysteries, past loves, traumas and human frailties, as he asked all of the right questions. In turn, I laughed and listened to the much more upbeat stories of his Swedish childhood, the trips to Lake Como in Italy and Skiing in Switzerland, and his days serving in the Swedish

Navy intelligence unit. I was thirsty to know more of this fascinating and wonderful man. Most relationships do follow this trend, by feverishly thirsting for as much information as we can have about this new person.

However, as they say, falling in love is easy; staying in love takes work. Sometimes, many years later, couples stop asking the vital questions. As we stop asking, we stop knowing. Resentment and loneliness take hold where love was once abundant. We assume we have all of the answers already, but the truth is, the answers to the questions change with time. How well do you know your beloved as they are right now? Not only the superficial facts, but also the deeper meanings that your partner's personal narratives hold for them. For instance, you might know that your partner just finished reading a self-help book on relationships. That is a fine and fancy; in fact, that shows you are listening, but what did they like about the book? How did the book help them understand something about relationships? Has this book changed anything about the way they view your relationship? That last one was a scary question! It makes us vulnerable to hearing something we may not enjoy hearing. Yet this terrain of vulnerability is where our relationship flourishes!

There is a mindfulness exercise, a walking meditation task that instructs us to simply walk forward, outdoors or indoors. As we place our footsteps upon our path, always with mindful precision, we notice the points of contact of our feet as they propel us forward. In doing this, we ground ourselves. With each step, we grow beyond ourselves. We take in and become one with everything around us. We encounter unchartered territories. When we are at our best, we practice mindfulness with each person or object we observe; we exercise active curiosity to others. It is called 'The Beginner's Mind.' When we think with our expert mind, we 'know' everything, and thus our first instance can become to see all of the problems in a scenario. We do this with our partners too. We imagine that we know what their response will be in a discussion, and what will trigger their irritations. When we use our beginner's mind, we are curious and aware of possibilities. Beginners are imaginative, and creative and aware of potential. In what ways have you stuffed your partner into a stale and suffocating box that doesn't fit with who they are in the present moment?

Imagine for instance that we are walking in a stretch of spongy emerald grass, moving towards a tree. When we are close to the tree we ask ourselves, *What is this?* Pause, stand for a long time and really think about this, the example of a tree. The answers are plenty: it is shade, it is a playground for climbing, it is wood, toothpicks, housing, safety, harbor from rain, a metaphor for strength—it's an oak. We can go as deeply and for as long as we like when our minds are truly present. Meeting each new person by leaving behind the belief that we already know what 'this' is, our minds glow with life. We already know it's the tree in our backyard, but we fail to grasp that the same tree becomes different in April and changes again in October. Time, weather, all cause everything around us to flux. If we stop perceiving, if we assume we know all of the 'other' around us, then we devitalize internally and our mindset causes everything around us to deaden as well.

Let us use this as an exercise to bathe our love with curiosity and an endless quest for greater understanding. So reflect and pause awhile and think of the many, many answers to the questions: "Who is this person, who is my spouse, who is my partner?" Create a list of 20 items. Start with their relationships to people around them. Who is important to them? What are their interests? What are their goals? What are their fears and disappointments? Then share this list with your partner. One of you at a time, talk about which things on the list feel very true for you and which things feel that they are a part of the outdated model of who you once were. Be very honest with each other through this, but be cautious of becoming angry or hurt over the lists. There is opportunity in this exercise. It will allow you both to go deeper into being together now.

Understanding and encountering our partner is a process which requires us to use all of our senses and abilities. We watch them and we observe with our eyes; we hear them and listen to their feelings. We should aim not only at listening with our ears but at listening with our hearts. Taking the process a step further, we not only hear but we seek to understand their thoughts and needs. We ask questions to deepen our understanding and we request greater knowledge. We touch and hold close their yesterdays and todays, and we look forward to tomorrow. It is in this way that understanding our partner is created.

As a mindful partner, we must take great pride in creating an atmosphere that increases the likelihood that our partner will feel safe enough to communicate their vulnerabilities. Time exerts a distinct effect upon our ability to share our true selves, even under the most nurturing and attentive circumstances. It usually takes several years for someone to trust their relationship enough to bring their most intimate secrets to the table. Until cresting the two year mark, many are a bit guarded and even defensive. All of this a product of the fear of being rejected. If you are being honest, you can think about what things you were afraid to tell your partner in the beginning of the relationship, for fear of being rejected. With time and trust, we open more. By being mindful of our responses to our partner, like a master weaver, we thread together and sustain an emotional climate that welcomes forever deepening discussions. If our partner attempts to share something and we don't slow down, tune in, and react in a way that exudes our ever present aspirational interest, warmth, and understanding, they may shut down temporarily or stop opening up at all. We will cover more in later chapters about how to mindfully connect and offer emotional support. It starts with the mindfulness tools of focused awareness and non-judgement.

To know your spouse means many things. We show interest by understanding the interpersonal patterns of our beloved. We seek to understand their way of being within relationships. Consider the question, how much personal space and time is ideal for them? We should acquire a sense of their humor. We attune to their fears so as to avoid traipsing about on their internal fears, and we hold them closely in consolation by doing our best to protect them from emotional or physical injury. Our daily efforts to connect with our beloved spouse is akin to taking a long, mindful inhalation each day. We vow to savor their essence. As we adopt the mechanisms of mindfulness, we will be more readily equipped to become suffused with the intoxication of them as the air we breathe. We use the mechanisms of mindfulness, to apply attention, our full senses to care for them. We are careful to know who is important to them and we do our best to support the relationships with others whom they care for. We come to understand what brings them joy and we do our best to provide some more contentment for them.

Ask your partner the above questions for two reasons: 1) so that you can understand them, and 2) so that they can feel understood. When they make statements, ask them to elaborate with questions like, 'Why is that important to you?' Probe the fundamentals, although be mindful that when we ask a simple question about a person that we may have spent years with, initially the basic nature of the inquiry can seem laughable. Yet, the longer we have spent time in a relationship with a person, the more important it is to use this mode of asking. In longterm marriages, we may be less likely to ask questions that ascertain valuable and current information. In fact, in working with couples, when we stop asking what kind of ice cream your partner prefers, our partner often interprets that as "she/he stopped caring." The person who stopped asking assumes that they know the answer to the question: *Of course I know Jerry's favorite ice cream; its vanilla bean with chocolate sauce.* Yet Jerry may reply something along the lines of, *Not since 85'—I stopped liking that long ago but you never asked.* The point is that our likes, interests, and hobbies are ever changing, and we must continually update our infographic of our partners' persona. We do this for each other in order to maintain an understanding of the person with whom we have a relationship. Our natural tendency to know and be close to our partner easily becomes outdated and can derail to a trajectory of turning away from each other instead of enjoying and sharing lives. Sometimes when we feel slighted or as though our partner isn't putting in as much effort as they should, we may decide that we will check out too. We purposefully lean out of our relationship; isolation chills the air when years of this behavior create a glacial effect on our once warm love.

We can do our best to create a life where being together isolates each of us from the tundra of loneliness out there. In fact, people who are in happy connected relationships even gain the benefit of longer healthier lives. In one study, the life span of happily married couples was found to be longer than that of single persons. The benefit of longevity was not found in unhappily married couples because they experienced earlier death and more sickness than single persons. Some of us, due to limited understanding, innate selfishness or childhood experiences enter partnerships where we think that love is all about getting our own selfish needs met. We expect to have a partner who lives up to some ideal version of the kind of person we believe we should be with; this is not love. Love is not about us.

You may be wondering at this point how well you do in fact know your partner. Please allow the following questions to be used as an opportunity to create greater understanding and awareness between you. Remember, understanding is created over time and with all senses. Hearing, speaking, touching are the ways in which our knowledge of our partner grows. Be gentle with each other and with yourself throughout the process. Use the mindful mechanism of non-judgement while you seek to deepen your awareness of each other.

Maybe you can zip through the below questions with ease. Even if you can, I encourage you to check your data and see how many of your answers do in fact match up to your partner. It is possible to use the questions between the two of you as an exercise to enhance awareness of each other and make it easier to address more important questions. By using it as a tool to spark creative dialogue, each partner should remember to remain open to the responses, to not become upset with each other when they do not know an answer, and to remember that this provides an opportunity to look a little more deeply.

Who was your partner's closest friend in childhood?

What was their childhood dream?

What was the biggest challenge she or he faced in childhood?

How did they manage or cope with that challenge?

What is your partner's biggest stress today?

How did you partner spend their day yesterday?

Who do they interact with on a daily basis?

What things are coming up in your partner's life that are important to them?

What are your partner's goals for the next year?

What are your partner's hobbies?

How have their hobbies changed over the years?

What is your partner's biggest fear?

How does your partner like to relax?

How does your partner deal with conflict?

What brings your partner joy and excitement?

What is your partner's favorite place to spend a vacation?

What is the most traumatic thing that has happened to your partner in his or her life?

How satisfied is your partner with the quality of your relationship together?

Who is your partner's closest friend or biggest source of support outside of the relationship?

Describe your partner's physical self.

Describe your partner's emotional self.

Describe your partner's spiritual self, or creative self if not spiritual.

Most of the above questions focus simply on knowing your partner and their basic life information. We do need to continually check-in with each other to see which answers are staying the same and which questions are now answered differently. Be actively curious, just like when encountering the tree. Be aware of how we respond to our partner in tone, volume, and choice of words so that we do our part in encouraging growing openness.

CHAPTER FOUR

MERGING—TWO WHOLE LOVERS ENCOUNTER EACH OTHER AND CREATE HARMONY TOGETHER IN A MINDFUL MARRIAGE

Creating a sacred and lifelong connection takes attention and devotion. As we note, all great beginnings start with a healthy and whole self. We have meandered along the lush and vibrant path to the deeper layers of being as an individual, entering into the seldom seen land of questions about the self, gaining the power of insight. With this current of self-knowledge carrying us, we are still not prepared to traverse the path to the beloved other. Our goal is to fully and with care encounter our beloved person with attentive interest, compassion, and full connection. With this encounter, the terrain around us changes while the journey unfolds for the two of us, who, hands entwined, continue our life walk, side by side. We attune to how we clasp each others' hands, taking notice of the points of contact, as well as the distances in the mindful merger of two distinct actualized persons who have joined together to form a "we".

The candy hearts of romance are not the hallmarks of marriage. Marriage is yard work and offering a tissue during cold and flu season. Lifelong love is the muddy and mundane and it is wonderful for being that. People don't commit to marriage for thrills and passion; they chose to remain committed each day because they honor their partner and value the consistent connection, care, and compatibility that they create together. If you are reading this book because you feel bored or disengaged, it is not because your partner has become dull. It is because you are looking outward for an enthusiasm that must come from within.

One of the most pivotal components of a relationship is to be self-actualized and to maintain the goal of acting in balance. A mindful merger that perches nestled in our outer-sanctum deliberately gravitates toward a healthy balance, and the weight of managing it is ours alone. There are a lot of 'all or nothing' people out there. Think about that friend you have that relationship-hops. Every month when you talk to them, it's a new idealized, perfect person who they can't seem to get enough of. Each month, it doesn't seem to work out for this friend and then it's back to the drawing board of idealizing the next match. This is not love. This is not meeting someone in balance. This is clinging to the hope that someone will rescue them. This is attempting to avoid loneliness and warding off the terror of abandonment.

In contrast, true love emerges with one who has shown their colors to be the right match. Only a person who is strong and whole and who has triumphed over their anxieties can love from wholeness. As mindful humans, we bear the weight of responsibility to actualize ourselves and co-create the landscape of our marriage with our partner. Our parents are not responsible for our misery. Our partner is not responsible for the issues we experience. The weight of responsibility falls directly upon you, the actor of your life. When we are awake and accountable, this is a sharp contrast to mindless acting. Blindly crawls the love of the child fumbling about to get its footing, still in the grips of childish defiance, unconscious of its motivations, propelled by impulse. The child is the person who reflexively says no to assert their will; the mature and loving adult looks for ways to say yes. I want to be influenced by my beloved. We grow to truly be aware of our values and needs. We evolve to learn the skill of loving another person. We choose the trajectory and accept the consequences of our choices, for better or worse.

This is distinctly different from any ordinary unmindful relationship that simply plods along, imagining that the relationship will simply manage itself in all of the hopeful years after 'I do.' Erich Fromm famously said that two people love each other in relation to the amount of loneliness that they felt before. While that is true, there may in fact be nothing lonelier than two people who live in the same home, but do not actively engage with each other on a consistent basis. A healthy relationship should be somewhat like a Venn diagram, two circles which partly overlap. Too much overlap and both feel entangled and unable to get a bit of air to breathe. Too little overlap, and they are adrift in the slow churning tide of aloneness. Some people enter a relationship and leave their friendships completely behind. They take no time to connect with former friends, and then at some point in the future, they wonder why they feel distinctly alone, despite having a wonderful well-tended relationship. We must have other people in our lives too. Another form of a relationship defect is when one or both partners live completely separate identities. A man I once knew was often seen around town, eating and drinking at all of the en vogue destinations. After years of a cordial friendship, I was surprised to learn that he was in fact married, but as nobody in our group of friends had ever met his partner, we could only further imagine just how fractured that marriage must be. This is the tightrope balancing act of merging and connecting, versus remaining rigidly whole as the self.

For what reasons do you and your partner connect with each other through the day? Parenting and sharing responsibilities are obvious areas where many couples note that they overlap—yet there is a marked aloneness in relationships that only converge in this area. Ask yourself or each other the questions below. If you are noticing that there are ideals that you have not yet achieved, you can be excited as this means there are many new places for your love to go as you further create the picture of what you want your relationship to be. After you take the time to write this for yourself, then make sacred time to sit with your partner and read your responses to the answers. Do this slowly; your partner is encouraged to ask questions to deepen their understanding. Both partners must commit to not be disappointed when learning about differences that exist between them.

Instead, you should have the mindset that each difference that is discovered is an opportunity to change and enhance your relationship.

How much closeness do you feel to your partner?

When do you feel closest to your partner?

When do you feel the most distance from your partner?

Describe the amount of time you spend with each other

What about the quantity of time you spend with your partner, would you like to be different?

What values do you share?

In what ways are you both most compatible?

On what are you and your partner currently collaborating?

What are two things that you really appreciate that your partner does for you?

How similar or different is this relationship to that of your parents' or childhood caregivers'? In what way?

What are some things that you and your partner fundamentally disagree upon?

In what ways do those differences get in the way or cause disagreements?

Can you imagine some ways that your disagreements could be resolved or managed differently?

How much time do you each spend in the relationship participating in activities with each other?

What is something new that you would like your partner to try with you?

How many in your social network of friends and family are shared friends?

What do you admire in your partner?

What is something you would like your partner to understand about you?

How well do you respect each other's needs for friends and time alone?

What is something that you wish your partner would do more of for themselves?

How well do you each collaborate and share tasks at home?

What is one thing you have been secretly or openly hoping to get more support from your partner on?

How do people in your lives view your relationship?

Do you know of a couple who has a very positive relationship?

What makes their relationship strong or ideal in your opinion?

What was your vision for this relationship when you entered it?

How does it feel in your body when you think of your answer to that question?

What is the scariest part about sharing this with your partner?

Is there anything that your partner can do to help reduce your fears?

When doing the reading and sharing portion of this exercise, it is most important to end with gratitude, by telling your partner, "Thank you for trusting me enough to share this." Remember lots of people say they want to go deeper into their relationship, but then they become defensive when they hear that there are things that their partner hopes, wants, or was saddened by. The attitude of defensiveness is not one where change will be cultivated, but instead will make any relationship stagnant and fearful.

The above questions help us to focus on what it means to be in a healthy relationship and to further examine the 'points of contact' in the Venn diagram of your precious love. All relationships are unique. You should be able to think of a few things about your relationship that do make it unique. Spend a few minutes to share those too. With the help of the above questions, you will start to take inventory of the quality of the mindful merger that you are experiencing so far. The following sections of the book are all devoted to sharing the skills of mindfulness which can help any couple to maintain and enhance their Mindful Merger. Even if you have not been practicing this kind of connection in your marriage, it is not too late to start now. Mindfulness and connection are skills that we can develop each day.

CHAPTER FIVE

COMMUNICATION, THE PATHWAY TO COMMUNICATING MINDFULLY

My husband and I, in our first phases of love, had come home from a party and started debating the merits of complementary compared to traditional western medicine. As the conversation heated up, Martin said, "but it's not based on evidence, it cannot be tested!" To some readers, this may sound basic and uneventful; yet for us, it is a trigger topic. I shut down, and attempted to storm off as he came thundering after me, "Where are you going? Don't leave!" My partner, fearing my abandonment, ensued. Now what had been anger for me immediately boiled over into panic, "Get away from me! I need to calm down!" With reserve and restraint that is typical of my husband now, he stepped back, making space for me to go for a long walk. My husband remains to this day aware of my core need—vital to our relationship health—that when in conflict, I need space to roam and cool down. What happened here? A communication failure in some ways and a relationship success in other ways. Let's use mindfulness and counseling theory to understand more deeply.

Communication holds the key to our potential by forging the path to connection. All of the methods for our intimate utterings allow an invisible thread to be cast from our feeling bodies and minds to that of our partner's. Spoken words cannot be seen, but they can be felt. They are the foundation of the intellectual and emotional parts of our relationship. Communication is a vital and hopeful conduit which instills our human potential with hope. It ushers us away from aloneness by providing ample opportunity for a well nurtured union. Communication can elevate us and be a mechanism to soothe those who we love. Communication can also tear us apart when used as weaponry to injure. For all of its possibilities, it can just as easily, perhaps at times even more easily than other means, turn friends into enemies. It is no wonder that communication is the number one issue that brings couples into marriage counseling.

Let's do a small exercise to build awareness; both you and your partner should write down the answers to these questions, and then after spending some time to think and becoming brave enough to be very honest, you should share your responses with each other. When you are sharing, ask your partner which of your self-insights are similar to their experiences with you. You should be looking for ways that your self-perception is different from your partner's perception of you. We often have limitations in how we see ourselves versus how others see us. We know we are doing good work if we start to catch some of those disparities. Notice, we are focusing on ourselves and our own style of communicating, as that is really the only aspect that we can control.

How would you describe your communication style in non-stressed, every day communication?

How did members of your family communicate when you were a kid?

Have you had or has any one in a prior relationship said they have had difficulties in communicating with you? What were they?

Do you enjoy and value communication, sharing as much as you can and as often as possible? Or, alternately, are you more stoic and reserved, a person who tries to process things autonomously?

In what situations do you notice yourself shutting down?

How do others respond to you when you are shut down?

Is it difficult for you to contain your thoughts and feelings?

How do others respond to you when you're communicating about emotionally fueled topics?

Can you share some times that it went well and times that communication didn't go well?

When you're upset, how do you communicate?

What is the hardest thing about communicating when you're upset?

Do you ask for breaks when you notice yourself being too overwhelmed to communicate effectively?

Do you prefer speaking or listening?

The spectrum of behavior that is embodied by communication includes a myriad of modalities that span listening, speaking, writing, body-language as well as facial cues or nonverbal communication. Ever see someone jumping up and down in the middle of the street, waving their hands and arms in the air? That's communication! The squeal of delight, the reaching for our partner's hand when entering a room full of strangers, that is communication too. The *How was I supposed to know that meant you wanted to leave?* kinds of moments can be greatly reduced as we work on our communication. From the tilt of the head to the sharp inhale of shock, communication, similarly to personality, starts to develop in childhood.

There are an abundance of factors that influence our style of communication, as well as our ability to understand the communication efforts of others. There are those, like many highly empathetic people and even counselors and other social scientists, who as a group score high on tests indicating their ability to perceive other's emotions. Also, as a group, those with autism spectrum disorder exhibit limitations in their ability to discern facial cues and social skills training is often a part of their therapeutic efforts. Then for all of the rest of people who are somewhere in between, and who want to apply greater learning to understand social cues, there are many strategies available to better understand what influences others and to find ways to communicate with them better. Our biology, our family interactions in childhood, and the way that we process our emotions are places that we may have less helpful communication strategies. We will examine how lovers communicate with their partner while in a cool state, how to manage your style of connecting when in the heightened emotional state of conflict, and how to incorporate mindfulness in each of these steps to increase your chances of understanding your partner and being better understood yourself.

Let us move toward the more targeted topic of Mindful Listening. All effective communicators know that this is the most important secret to successful understanding. It all starts with listening attentively and actively, providing undivided attention to our partner. It has rapidly become a common topic on the couples counselors' couch: Imagine, two well intentioned people flop down on the couch. The woman folds her arms over her chest, peeling her slitted eyes over to her partner when asked what brings them in to counseling. "He never listens to me!" Every good counselor will ask, "Well what does that mean, never listens to you? When do you feel most unheard?" Most of the time the answer is, "He is always on his phone!" This can just as easily be applied to all genders, because we are all guilty of it sometimes. We call them well-intentioned misses because that is exactly what they are. Most of the time, it is not a sinister action like an affair or porn addiction that keeps others pasted to their personal device; it is social media, work, or even texting friends. So common is this relationship error that there is a new psychological vocabulary being created around it. To snub someone with your cell phone is called, 'phubbing.' If you really want to become a master listener, the first step is to tune in by putting your phone down, turning off your television, and turning your body and eyes toward the person who is speaking. We must be able to prioritize our partner when they come into a room wanting to share something with us. Yet it will be a struggle. I can attest that for me it is also a struggle. When my dear husband comes bursting into the room ready to exuberantly share the highlights of his day, "My talk went really well!", there are times I can barely hear him because I have my phone in hand. I am absorbed in firing back to a client or managing some need that my team has. My gaze may not even move toward him. That is how focused some of us can become when we are in a workflow. At times, this has led to arguments between us. My husband, irritated by my lack of attention, having to compete with the email app on my phone, might even sputter, "Stephanie, put down the phone!" Of course then I get irritated that his voice is raised and I am more than ready to shout my response, "Do not yell at me!" There it is; we are off to the races, arguing about nothing. Instead, when practicing good relationship skills, we listen by focusing and encouraging their engagement.

We should note the difference between active and passive listening. Passive listening happens when you might be hearing but the speaker isn't necessarily noticing that you are. In the example of my own poor listening above, I could have been hearing, but the speaker feels completely rejected and unheard. Active listening means that we have focused awareness of our partner when they are talking, *and we are also cuing with our body language that we are interested* by perhaps head nodding and maintaining a relaxed expression on our face. As our lover speaks, we may follow up with questions to indicate our interest in what they have shared. We shouldn't assume that we understand. We should use our active interest to guide our efforts in moving toward our partner by asking for clarification about the informational layer of what has been stated. Even if our partner is going on about something that is not of interest to us, we should do our best to ask some questions about it. Questions don't only provide us with more information, they provide our partner with an opportunity to talk about something that is important to them.

You see, take note of this point, *speaking has a purpose for both the listener and the speaker.* They both get something valuable. For instance, a part of therapy's value is that we gain a different form of insight when our thoughts are spoken, and when someone, a therapist, or our partner asks questions to deepen the conversation, the speaker can even start to think about the issue differently. To strengthen your relationship, this means sharing in a dialogue of questions and creating opportunities to enhance positive interaction by using the skill of active listening. You will soon notice that when you and your partner are bonding and sharing the neutral and brighter moments of life, attention is always tuned in this way. When you become mindful of providing this kind of care to your partner, it can become relatively easy to achieve. As we noted, the most common barrier to active listening is inattention caused by distractions. We get so caught up in achieving, working, children, and family that we check out a bit and may start to miss the opportunities for asking questions and experiencing the bond created by mindful listening.

Above we mentioned the importance of asking questions. When we focus, it should be relatively easy to ask questions about aspects outside of the relationship. Yet, as we will see, it becomes tremendously difficult when we attempt to discuss a problem *within* the relationship. It is vitally important to tune in and ask for more understanding when we are discussing our partner's needs in the relationship. We must use mindfulness to regulate our emotions and to steer away from the heightened emotional states of anger which can lead to poor communication and defensiveness, preventing us from being able to listen to our partner's attempts to create dialogue about interrelation topics. We will delve into calm emotional reactivity in the later section of this chapter, highlighting triggers, as well as communicating about them, such as in the instance I shared about my husband and I in our disagreement. It is of vital importance.

There are many couples who say that they want to communicate better or that their partner doesn't share pieces of vital information. For these individuals who are hoping for more, imagine what *you* might be doing that could contribute to this, as will be the typical train of thought throughout this book. If you feel that your partner knows everything about you, that doesn't mean that you know everything about them. Some of the best communicators are terrible listeners, so transfixed they are with the sound of their own voice. Other times, maybe we are asking our partner the right questions, and providing them some moments to form a response, but we must also be mindful about the way we respond to our partner when they do open up and share their thoughts. Imagine the following situation: Our partner comes to us and says, "You know, I have been feeling really distant from you." We respond by turning to them with a flushed face, and through clenched teeth sharply say, "What you do mean by that? How could you say that? We were just together at lunch yesterday!" In this example, the amount of fiery defensiveness becomes a barrier to understanding what is happening for our partner. The partner above was trying to open conversation about how she was feeling and she was also taking a risk in coming closer to her partner, yet the risk was not well rewarded. Instead of achieving mutual understanding, she was rebuffed. Most likely she will not bring up the subject again and she will instead stifle her feelings of aloneness while continuing to feel disengaged from her partner. Let us look at how we can calm our emotions and respond to the scenario just described with mindfulness instead of hostile defensiveness.

Begin by thinking about how much your partner communicates with you regarding his or her needs, thoughts, concerns, or just daily life.

How much to you talk throughout the day?

Are your communications text? Calls? In person talks?

What would you like to improve about the frequency of communication between you?

What are a few things that happened to your partner that they were happy about?

Do you know of a few things that have happened recently within the relationship that annoyed your partner?

How did your partner communicate about the annoyances?

How did you respond to your partner when they shared their annoyances?

If you are saying yes to some of the above, take it as a sign of relational health! It's a very good thing if your partner has shared some joyful things with you and an even better thing if they have shared their annoyances with you. How can it be a good thing that they shared their annoyances you might be asking? Well, simply, that means they care about the relationship and feel hopeful about your willingness to invest in making changes. Now, if you answer no to all or some of the above, let us look at the ways you may be contributing to the lack of connection with verbal and non-verbal communication. This isn't to say that it is completely your fault if your partner doesn't communicate well. They may have an avoiding style of communication, fear of intimacy, a tendency to speak passive aggressively, mask their concerns in humor, or an overall anxiousness that contributes to this avoidance of talking about their needs or concerns. We cover much more about this in later chapters. Beyond talking about any of those above mentioned potential contributing factors, we will look at what you can do to enhance connection communication. Let us explore further, when your partner has raised an issue do you:

> Do you pay attention to your partners' words?
>
> Do you listen for subtle and even direct requests?
>
> What facial expressions do you adopt when your partner is communicating? Do you scrunch in your eyebrows, become elevated in tone or defensive of the content being shared?
>
> What is your feeling state—meaning how do you feel when your lover brings up a problem topic? Are you reactive or receptive? Do you shut it down and tell them that it isn't possible? Do you reflexively try to convince them that they are wrong for thinking this?

If you are starting to notice that your common way of responding to your partner, like in the above scenario, is to become hostile, aggressive or classically defensive, keep reading. You have already achieved the first step in mindfulness, which is to pay attention to what you are doing. We will delve into this topic more deeply in the coming chapters and learn ways that effectively change our experiences and the outcome of our relationships.

CHAPTER SIX

SPEAKING MINDFULLY

The second part of Mindful Communication is about to how we speak or communicate our thoughts, feelings, needs, and desires. Our manner of speech is the foundation and building block upon which every micro bit of understanding between our partner and ourselves is founded. What we say and how we say it, including our content, tone, and its resonance, may unveil layers of meaning that we didn't even intend for it to disclose.

Notice the difference between the statements, *Close the door now!* versus *Can you please help me by closing the door?* There are so many subtle tones that alter the way our speech is perceived. We have all been there, trying to make some point about the what we need from our partner and they end up upset, only to leave us wondering, *How did this go here? I did not mean to be critical or offensive!* Furthermore, how we communicate to our partner and how they in turn respond to us has a direct effect upon the entire rest of the way we think, feel, and relate to our relationship. Meaning, when we have so many exchanges where we end up feeling misunderstood, we start to change the way we feel about our love. We may start to think that the relationship isn't such a good one or that it is doomed to fail. Verbal exchanges have a both cognitive and emotional aspect to them. How we feel is related to how we speak, and how we speak also affects how we and our partner and family feel. We call this a feedback loop. Most interactions have some sort of feedback loop.

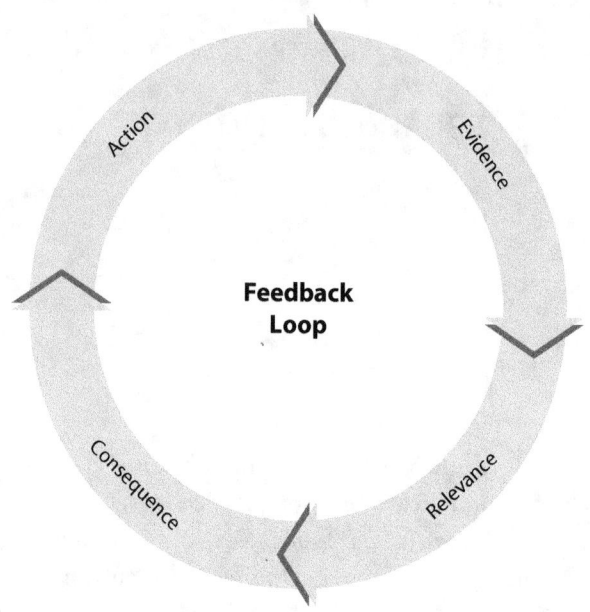

It may be very difficult to think that we are responsible for the outcome of much of our current unhappiness and hurt. However, the actions which we choose affect our daily lives, and nowhere is this more evident than in communication. In fact, according to research done by the Gottman Research institute, 96% of the time, we can predict where a conversation will go based upon how it starts.

There are some people who have reached the master level of mindful communication, meaning that they naturally move toward being clear, constructive, curious, and nurturing in the way that they initiate conversations with their partners. These effective communicators are also gentle but direct in the way that they respond. By doing so, they draw a crisp road map to their spouses by explaining their needs and feelings in a non-threatening way in order to further yield clarity and understanding. It takes ample practice to become fluid and dynamic in creating such relational synergy with our partner.

It also takes practice in understanding our own emotions so we can talk about what we are feeling. Some people spend their whole lives attempting to avoid thinking about and sharing the deeper layers of their emotional selves.

Think for a bit about the layers of things that we can speak about

Informational—The informational layer is any statement that expresses a need or a fact. For example, when we ask our spouse or partner to pick up milk on the way home from work, we are making a request and exchanging information. We talk about the timeline of our day, we make plans for our next family trip. These are all informational exchanges. Imagine that our partner comes in from a long day and in monotone defeat states, "I lost my job." This is informational; we now know the 'what,' but the statement doesn't expose the emotion of our partner's experience at all. If expressed this way, we may be tempted to dismiss or minimize the information. If we change the subject or start talking about how much we know what that is like because we too have lost a job, we miss this relationship moment. It is imperative to ask questions to draw out more from our partner, more of the feelings behind the statement. When a person fails to ask questions to deepen their understanding of what is being communicated to them, much is lost. It is very common for couples to come into therapy and say that they 'feel like roommates' with their partner. One of the things that they mean by this statement is that their communication primarily falls on the level of exchanging bits of observation by relaying facts, planning simple goals, and executing the administrative business of living life together. Some relationships get by just fine remaining on this layer. Problems arise when one person yearns for a different kind of interaction with their partner and the other either doesn't know how to give it or refuses to learn. The fact is, by delving into the feelings behind the daily interactions we have, we enter a different layer of depth with our beloved.

Emotional—An exchange of emotional information is the magical zest that clears the way to deeper understanding. It is also when we ask about our partners' feelings that we unearth more about how they are truly feeling and who they are in that moment. The truth is, sharing feelings can be scary, and receiving an emotionally charged statement can even overwhelm the listener. In love and closeness, we share joys and suffering with the hope of experiencing some degree of empathy and emotional understanding. To continue to illustrate the above example, notice the difference in expression: "I am so distraught and overwhelmed; I lost my job and I don't know what I am going to do." This phrasing is not focused only on information as in the previous example. Here the statement incorporates the feeling spectrum. When we share our feelings with another, it can elicit complex reactions. Feelings are not always met with openness in our culture; our society prizes facts and dismisses emotions. Men are taught to not share their feelings less they be thought of as 'girly' or less masculine. The cumulative effect is that men are raised to be at a disadvantage in emotional expression and even have exhibited deficits in emotional vocabulary. In other instances, for men who do remain expressive of their emotional sentiments, others can be critical or shaming of this. Yet, most of us crave more emotional exchange without knowing how to define it. It is definitely a challenge for some of us to give and receive the emotional portion of the content that we communicate. The feeling layer of communication is nestled in a deeper stratum and it has the potential to exhibit vulnerability. Yet, every time we allow ourselves to be vulnerable, we also gain the rich potential for deeper bonding.

Continuing our exploration into the depths of communication, we now land upon *meaning*. When we convey or understand what something means to our partner, we unearth layers of content and feeling terroir. Through those mounds of information, we harken to the deepest layer that resonates with human reasoning. Whether it is personal meaning, universal meaning, or both of them, it requires a self-actualized person shrouded in safety to get to this space. The paradise of closeness is ours when we communicate on this level.

Let us continue with the example of losing one's job: "I lost my job today. I don't know what I will do. I am terrified I am going to turn out like my dad. I remember watching him sit at home with no purpose year after year while our family struggled to make ends meet." Now we glean the vicissitude of significance attached to the loss. We are not able to have this kind of intimate exchange with a stranger—it is the plane of true intimacy. To make the statement above, the person is expressing and sharing an extraordinary level of self-awareness. It takes work to get there and trust that your statement will be received in a non-judgmental way.

One other form of communication which deserves mention is Meta-communication. This is about our ability to think, reason, and feel. It might sound like a riddle or a tongue twister, but it means that with all of our brain's capacity, we can think *about thinking* and feeling. We can talk about our thinking and feeling much like this whole text and many other texts are devoted to. Meta-emotion and meta-communication is on the same layer of existence as mindfulness. It is a growing awareness of the level of our communication, our emotions, and our thoughts—both internal and external. Ironically, this meta layer can also be a source of disagreement.

When couples argue, they are sometimes rehashing misunderstandings in the layers of meta communication. For instance, a few weeks ago, my husband and I were at a barbeque and he started to tell our group of friends that we had a disagreement earlier in the day. He described to the group how I was complaining about the frequency of his golfing. I became upset and talked with him about this later. I explained that it makes me very uncomfortable for our disagreements to be the centerpiece of the group discussion and I was especially hurt by his sharing this as I had expressed my regret in not handling the situation in the calmest way. The argument intensified as he rebutted, "I wasn't saying it in an offensive way, it's no big deal!" This invalidation became the landslide. As we went back and forth, we slid further away from agreement. As a counselor, I was able to use the understanding of meta-communication to stop the argument from progressing by explaining to my husband, "this is defensiveness.

I don't need for you to tell me that my perception is not accurate or not what you intended; I need you to see and understand my perspective." When we take a step back and think about the ways in which we communicate with our partner, we are in the meta zone. Meta-communication has abundant potential to create change, as we become aware of how we can do something about our patterns from within ourselves and within our relationship interactions. Stepping out of the heated moment, seeing what is happening and becoming empowered to make changes, this is it, this is everything that mindfulness is about.

Chapter Challenge: Challenge yourself and your relationship to this exercise for one week. First, tune into which kinds of communication you and your partner are having. Now that you have become very inquisitive about the kinds of communication that exist, take a note pad and make columns with Informational, Emotional, Meaning, and Meta-Communication. After each communication with your partner for a week, make a check next to the column with one word topic for each different type. At the end of 7 days, talk about it. You will very likely observe a lot of information exchanges, but if you are both balanced and healthy in your approaches to emotional wholeness and communication, then you should have at least 10% of the meaning and feeling conversations. If you are not observing any meaning and feeling statements, then use the following prompts to incorporate more of the deeper forms of communication into your relationship's dialogue. Ask more questions like the following when your partner shares some bit of information. Also remember, these questions deepen the conversation. They are not to be squandered or doled out when we think there is an opportunity to go deeper in the conversation; we create the depth by using these questions in ordinary moments:

How does this make you feel?
What is the hardest part about this?
How can you manage this in a way that will make you feel proud in the future?

Does this remind you of anything else you have ever been through?

Does this remind you of anything that you saw happen in your home as a child?

What do you make of this situation?

What does this mean to you?

How does this affect the way you think and feel about yourself?

How does this affect the way other people might look at you?

What kind of person do you aspire to be?

In what ways are you living up to your version of success?

In what ways do you want to grow?

Communication is one of the most common concerns that couples identify as a reason that they seek therapy. It has the capacity to be a bonding agent that can enhance and strengthen our love. It can also be a source of insidious confusion which provides ample opportunity for misalignment and misunderstanding. There are certain themes which unsuccessful attempts at communication have in common. In the next chapter, we will examine some of the mechanisms which are barriers to having fluid and constructive communication.

CHAPTER SEVEN

FROM EMOTIONAL REACTIVITY TO MINDFULNESS IN COMMUNICATION

Ideally, we share a thought or feeling to be understood, and we ask questions to learn more about the internal world of our partner. We state our needs and discuss our emotions in order to create opportunities for enhancing our relationship and enjoying the safe haven of emotional support. When we share a need, thought or feeling, we should keep in mind our goal, which hopefully is to be understood or to solve a problem, not to hurt or control our partner. It is appropriate that we expect a response to our statement, this response being our feedback loop. Yet it is also true that we must use the skill of stating our thoughts constructively and ask for help in a way that is gentle and non-attacking. When we belittle, blame, and criticize our beloved, we launch an aggressive style of communication that entices more conflict. When we utilize aggression in words and feelings, our partner will either shut down, tune out, or attack back. When we are communicating in a space that is emotionally charged, clinically, we can prompt this emotional reactivity.

Aggressive communication is indeed hurtful and confusing, but some of the most hurt individuals who come for counseling are those whose partners ignore their attempts at communication. It is true that we communicate with both what we say and with what we don't say:

silence too speaks volumes. Let us look at a vignette. Imagine Kate and Simon: Kate walks into the kitchen and notices that the garbage bin is overflowing—a common enough scenario for many couples. She is angry as her partner had promised to take out the trash on Tuesday morning. Over the years, the topic of cleanliness is something that she and her partner have repeatedly talked about. She **reacts** to her anger and marches over to her husband, forging a loud and demanding complaint about not taking out the garbage. She enters into a tirade along the lines of, "What's wrong with you? You never empty the trash bin! I can't take this anymore." Simon mumbles something inaudible with his arms crossed over his chest, the words and response clouded by the haze of his emotions. A deafening silence permeates the room. He lowers his head. Kate already feels ignored, frustrated, unheard, and she interprets her partner's silence as evidence of his coldness and lack of caring about her. Remember that in her world, the true goal of her communication is to communicate her feeling, and to get her partner to move toward change. Simon who was the recipient of the attack feels diminished, overwhelmed, and equally frustrated. Kate may walk away or raise her voice and tone, further escalating the argument, and the whole garbage can issue risks veering toward a dangerous screaming match. This is what sometimes happens when we feel unheard. We begin to cry louder and louder. Ironically, the louder we speak, the less likely it is that we will achieve any understanding in our communication. How different this could have been if both partners had been using these mindfulness strategies. The speaker could have taken notice of the frustration of feeling unheard, and paused to find calm instead of reacting to her anger over the neglect of the household chores. Understanding and compassion can be reached by using mindfulness and maintaining composure instead of reacting with a gush of emotion.

I can assure you, after working with thousands of couples and reviewing the evidence of volumes of research that it is true that both of the above persons are in a "fight or flight" state of mind. Although it may not at first appear completely obvious, many of those who become either noisy with fury or quiet in stony defensiveness during conflict are so overwhelmed that their ability to reason shuts down completely. The science behind mindfulness teaches us that when we are in the state of hyper-arousal, our autonomic functions crescendo to heart rates of over 100 bpm. Have you ever tried to see your reflection in a pond rippled by the force of a huge wind? Vision is cloudy at best during times of turbulence. It is common for marriage counselors to use oximeters in their sessions with couples and unfailingly they exhibit this pattern of sky high heart rate during the conflict discussions. It is because their adrenal glands are dumping cortisol into their bloodstream, fueling their bodies' ability to run great distances. This is what is meant by fight or flight. The undesired effect of heightened emotional states is that when all of our energy is shifted into fueling our organs and limbs to run, we have depleted our capacity for higher-order reasoning. However, the cool state of mind, which is available when we are unperturbed, provides the best opportunity for the strategic reasoning that is required to solve our marital conflicts. Interestingly, to resolve fight or flight, our bodies require from us either an ample amount of self-soothing or a 'time-out' period. Time out allows us to recalibrate towards achieving the reserve of internal calm. Later, when we have reclaimed some measure of our inner stillness, our rational and constructive goals can be re-approached with the hope of mutual collaboration. While most everyone can relate to being emotionally upset, some of us have a greater range of emotional variability while others remain rather steady, perhaps becoming emotionally activated after only very serious infractions. Still other types are often trembling on the edge of emotional disturbance and it takes very little to push them over the edge. For a person who doesn't have the same tendency toward emotional reactivity, it may be a challenge to imagine what the sensation of fight or flight is like. Think about being in a boat that is braving the high swell of the ocean seas, the boat churning and rocking about. Your whole body may become nauseous and just keeping your feet planted on the deck requires massive concentration. Emotional reactions can be that way. We lose our ability to focus on the distance of the horizon or to zoom out to see the big picture, the meta picture of what is happening, so we can act on that information. Instead, our motions and sight are deadened with the force of the gale winds as our vessel careens, just managing to stay afloat without capsizing, or we flail our arms about as we become submerged in the turbulent surrounding water.

If you are a person or part of a couple who is especially prone to become activated with heightened emotion during conflict, best practice indicates that both you and your partner should form a plan for how to disengage when emotions become acute. An effective method involves the following four steps:

1) Check in and label your emotional state to yourself. We must first be aware of our own emotions for any of our efforts toward mindfulness to be helpful. State to yourself first, "I feel _____."

2) Then realize and internally state to your partner the need to disengage from the dialogue.

3) Share the need to disengage with your partner in a gentle and respectful way by stating: "I am not in a good problem solving or understanding state of mind; I need to cool down for 20 minutes." (You can take more time if you need it up to 24 hours.)

4) Re-engage when both of you feel calm enough, keeping in mind the goal of mutual understanding and compromise when the conversation begins again.

The key is to have formulated this conflict management plan in advance when both of you are in a cool state and agree to use this method to reduce your heated arguments. By using this format, the person who needs space to calm down is given a time to re-engage conversation so that the person who is providing the space does not feel shut out or abandoned, but is merely activating this plan. Many of the most destructive arguments are preventable. We can manage to find our way back to mutual communication by noting that we are internally angry, hurt, upset, and acknowledging our need to take a small break from the disagreement to regain our emotional balance.

Conflict management plans are indispensable for long time relationships as well as new ones. Both persons should respect the need for space and do their best to keep in mind the goal of better understanding when they re-engage in a conversation aimed at creating mutual understanding and compromise. The shores of shared understanding will be reached when the sea of emotions calms down, later on.

Mindfulness, in addition to de-escalating conflict, can also become the antidote to prevent our attempts at communication from descending the landslide of mutual hurt and irritation that was illustrated in the attempted dialogue above. As we nurture our relationship with ourselves, the most important component of our journey toward mindful relatedness is to identify our own feelings and the feelings of our partner. What do we feel? It takes practice to look at what we are feeling and to be honest with ourselves about it. You wouldn't believe how much work it sometimes takes for people to notice the signs of their own anger or acknowledge the vulnerability of mutual hurt. Ever stand in the face of a person who is screaming at you with clenched fists, "I am not angry!" After identifying our feelings, we do a mindfulness breathing exercise, or other time tested grounding technique to regulate our emotions. We regulate those emotions so that we are sure we are not falling into the pitfall of reactivity.

Our goal is to go from being reactive to our emotions to reflective when sharing our needs and moving toward our mutual relationship goals. If each time that we feel irritated with our partner we attack and spew venom, we will not be productive in influencing our lover or understanding them. Sometimes when we have the kind of personality that consistently trembles on the threshold of heightened emotive frequency, it takes more work to reach the state of non-reaction. It is a psychological and scientific fact that some people really do feel more than others; they are dubbed 'super feelers'. They are wired with more mirror neurons and heightened reactivity in the amygdala. This increases the importance of taming the inner fire and noticing the ways that one can be prone to over-communicate or to communicate in a way that enhances the likelihood of conflict. We must use mindfulness to get out of the loop of reactivity and deconstructive conflict and shape this new pathway where we are mindful of ourselves, our thoughts, feelings, and goals. Remember, mindfulness observes inner irritation but doesn't judge ourselves for it; it is ok to be irritated with our partner sometimes. It is ok to be distracted at work sometimes. We must accept our imperfect nature as the first step toward becoming our best selves. We must acknowledge that our relationship is also not perfect; we will still have disagreements and arguments, but the key to adopting mindfulness is that we begin to fight fair.

Another reality on the opposite end of the spectrum is that our relationships isn't always bursting with excitement. Some of us become very bored or anxious when encountering the quietude, peace, or the doldrums of the relational spectrum. Imagine a woman, Christine. She and her partner Ed were married for 2 years when they entered counseling for their frequent bouts of conflict. During their treatment, the counselor analyzed some of their history and noted that most of their greatest disagreements happened during periods of what might be celebratory hallmarks for other couples. For instance, when they became engaged, Christine was caught texting a former partner in a lurid manner. On the day they moved in together, Christine became furious with Ed about the shape of the closets so much that she stopped the move completely that day and forced the movers to place all of her belongings back in her former house. The therapist started to wonder if some of this self-sabotaging behavior came from the terror of boredom that Christine previously exhibited.

Lots of people don't know how to sustain intimacy; they are only acquainted with the pattern of pushing away and coming back together. Others use conflict to create an adrenaline rush in the relationship. Mindfulness as adopted in the therapeutic plan is the first step to overcoming these tendencies. Even when we are with our ideal perfect match, we will have disagreements, we will feel the plethora of emotional responses, at times ecstatic, soothed, overjoyed, and irritated, hurt, frustrated, and bored. Mindfulness serves as a pathway which honors all emotions, but doesn't attempt to extinguish the wisdom contained in the breadth of our emotions. We learn to respond to our own and our partner's feelings in a way that enhances our relationship. Mindfulness does hold the key to enhancing our verbal exchanges in a way that reinforces the overall fabric of our relatedness by sustaining enriched, connected love. It should always be noted that we must enter every single conversation by first reminding ourselves of the goal of maintaining peace and collaboration.

The second step after doing our mindfulness self-soothing routine is to spend some time in a neutral, non-reactive state, figuring out what it is that we **need** from our partner. This too will be very hard for most of us to do. I can assure you that communicating mindfully and refraining from making critical or argumentative statements takes great effort and coaching for the couples who I work with. Imagine we come home from a hike outdoors to our partner seated on the couch, arms crossed over their chest. Before you can make your way over to them to say hello, they say, "You are always off on private retreats; you are never home anymore!" Before reacting to their criticism, we might ask ourselves or them, what does our partner need from us right now? What are they feeling? I would proffer that they are begging for more conversation and more connection, and is consequently feeling overwhelmed and possibly unheard. As we learn to use the strategies of mindfulness and attempt communication by stating our feelings and needs clearly and constructively, the outcome will be dramatically different.

This brings us to an exercise to complete individually. Mentally index the last five disagreements that you had with your partner and think about what your need was. Keep in mind that a need isn't a negative statement like the following: *I need him to quit forgetting the trash.* The need here is *more help in emptying the trash.* That is still a critical and aggressive statement. A need provides a positive opportunity to be met with collaboration. A need provides hope for change. So, go ahead and give it a try while remaining optimistic. Getting it right takes some time and practice! What are the five disagreements and what were your needs?

As you continue to adopt greater mindfulness concerning your needs, you will more deeply understand yourself and be able to sympathize with your motivations while finding better methods to achieve them. The outcome is that we can interact with our partner in a way that is constructive and hopeful. The goal will be to use this format to communicate with your partner about the things that happen between you. This interaction steers completely clear of the relationship destroyers of emotional reactivity and the quarrelsome factors of criticism and blame.

CHAPTER EIGHT

MINDFUL SELF-CARE AND SELF-SOOTHING STRATEGIES

We do know that a part of having a great relationship is knowing how to manage ourselves and our emotional tides. We should have a plan for de-escalating ourselves and turning away from conflict to calm down when something happens outside of the relationship or inside of the relationship. It might be easier to manage the plan for what we do when something flips our world upside down that comes from outside of the relationship. When for example your cherished dog dies, you might likely attempt to rely on your partner for support. When you and your partner are disagreeing and the turbulence comes from inside the relationship, it might not be practical to rely on your partner for support in that moment, or perhaps you are a person who prefers to regulate your emotions in solitude. No matter the case, your unique plan must include coming back to talk about the issue when you are calm again. As a part of emotional hygiene, we should form our protocol for finding calm. This will be a highly personal endeavor, so take the time to personalize it for yourself. Include at least two or three different strategies in your self-soothing routine. It will serve as your protocol to be mindful of encountering the flurries of irritation that will inevitably arise between you and your partner. Remember, invariably our objectivity is heightened as our emotions are de-escalated, and this is when we will do our best mutual problem solving. Let's look at some of the best exercises that couples and individuals use to enhance their emotional health and balance.

Deep Breathing—Mindfulness deep breathing exercise or diaphragmatic breathing meditation starts by finding or creating a comfortable place. Some people have a favorite room in their house, or even outdoors in nature can be a serene and peaceful setting. Others who have practiced meditation for a long time may create a special altar in their home which is specifically designated to house their meditation practice. When we are doing our meditation or deep breathing practice, we should do at least 5 to 10 minutes of long, slow, deep, inhalations for a count of 6 and then equally controlled, long, slow exhalations for a count of 8. The added benefit of this measured breathing is that it down-regulates the heart rate and diffuses the fight or flight that we discussed previously. When executing an exhalation that is incrementally longer than the inhalation, the parasympathetic nervous system is activated and reins in the sympathetic nervous system. With meditation and deep breathing, we practice our physical ability to mindfully move our bodies out of the arousal state of fight or flight to the calm state of rest and digestion.

Grounding techniques can be practiced along with breathing. This is where you will put your attention on the seat beneath you, the floor supporting your feet, notice the air on your skin and the clothing on your skin. Grounding puts you closer into yourself as you again allow your attention to graze your physical experience.

Fitness is a premium and highly effective addition to other self-care strategies and particularly effective for managing emotions. Actually, any physical activity helps, including cardio, walking, running, and even dancing. While seeking an activity for refuge to give ourselves the time and space needed to activate calm after a disagreement, exercise in any form that provides ample catharsis to discharge some of the heightened energy that you may be feeling.

Nature: A third way to activate calm after conflict communication is by spending some time outdoors in nature, which has fantastic health benefits for us. In one study, cortisol levels were compared in two groups of people, one which had taken a long walk in a city and another which took a walk in nature. While the exercise of walking was the same, those who took their walk in nature had significantly lower cortisol levels. This helps us to understand that there is something innately soothing about nature that beats stress. Remember to tune into the sights, sounds, and smells of the outdoors, and bring your total focused awareness to what is around you. Think about what your favorite outdoor setting is; is it a lush vibrant forest? A quickly moving stream? A placid remote pond? Even a freshly manicured golf course can arguably place us outdoors in a way that is soothing.

Friends: Talking to a trusted friend or relative is another way that we can sooth ourselves and manage emotions. Some of us really do best by reaching out to others for an open ear when we feel emotional stress. Make a list of three or four people whom you trust and will not mind if you turn to them as a friend when you are upset. Also, you should have a protocol for what you can do if you are not able to reach your support network when you need it. That may include some of the other strategies we have already mentioned.

Journaling is another tool that can be cathartic in times of emotional stress. This is quite valuable when you have many thoughts milling about that might not be appropriate to state to your partner. Recording them on paper with no judgement or audience allows you to empty yourself of those thoughts without saying things that you may later regret. It can also be a thought provoking exercise to later look back on those words and ask yourself, what did you need from your partner in that moment? Looking back, how would you have felt if you had made those statements when in the heat of disagreement?

Singing probably sounds silly, but the act of singing actually brings joy and happiness and there is a stress relieving opportunity in allowing sound to resonate from the belly. The tone needn't be a gleeful sound, but can be baritone or rapid to release the energies you are attempting to suppress.

Art: Drawing, painting, coloring all can be used to calm oneself. You needn't be a Picasso either as many companies have even made adult coloring books available. They are specifically formulated to help with emotional management.

Gardening is another way that many people find their inner calm. It has the benefit of also placing the gardener out in nature but with the targeted focus that comes with weeding and planting. It is no wonder that many great zen masters were known to practice the art of gardening and bonsai. It is a true mindful experience to cut and prune away the pieces of plants, to let go of what is no longer striving and uproot that which stands in the way of our planted friend's growth.

Baking and cooking in general can be quite cathartic. I mention baking first because doing things like kneading dough are both physical and full of concentration. Plus they yield delicious outcomes which are much more savory than standing around fuming at our beloved partner.

Blowing Bubbles while often associated with childhood, it is a practice which brings attention to the breath and inspires deep concentration so that your mind is no longer retracing the footsteps of the activating disagreement. Plus, they are lovely to watch as they dance toward the clouds.

Pottery: Similar to bubbles, many people love to mold clay when they are stressed. It becomes a tangible object to touch and anything that involves tactile stimulation is a great way to ride waves of emotions to calm down.

Practicing any diversion is a great way to regulate emotion, including reading a book, or even watching television—or something else entirely as long as it has personal meaning to you. It can be any activity that holds your attention and distracts you from continuing to think about a disagreement for twenty or thirty minutes. Some of us erroneously imagine that when we practice a diversion, we are avoiding the discussion. This is not true. Engaging in an activity to create greater calm for ourselves is far different from avoiding our feelings or not managing our relationship. The goal is to reach the non-reactive state, the calm space where we can provide ourselves and our loved one optimal presence and understanding in order to solve our problem issue. The biggest challenge that couples cite when they enact a plan for emotional management is actually using the plan. It takes great effort, but all couples who do exercise their ability to practice self-soothing are benefited greatly.

CHAPTER NINE

THE RISK OF COMMUNICATION AVOIDANCE AND INACTIVITY

Another communication style that is in stark contrast to reactivity is inactivity. The risks related to non-communication are great. Two persons who used to love each other experience a cool chill where there was once warmth, the quiet and distance like a gleaming iceberg between them. In this kind of relationship, there is no or little communication about feelings or meaning. Typically, the remnants of their exchanges are centered around information about basic survival, co-parenting and administration of household duties. This communication style is in direct opposition to the couples who seek therapy for too much argument. It is a red flag when couples state, "We never argue." This means that the couple also potentially doesn't engage with each other's inner worlds much at all. Instead, they report feeling isolated and completely unaware of each other's daily life and needs. This type of relationship can slide by for many years as there is no identifiable issue to pinpoint. Instead, there is the grim shadowy outline of boredom, pale loneliness, and opaque discontent which is the natural consequence of drifting away from supportive connection and spiraling towards distance.

If you are wondering how two people can end up in that situation, there are several other reasons that lead to intimate communication failure. First, some people are passive in communication by nature. Second, some people simply avoid intimacy. They are only able to let a partner enter their internal world in minute doses before retreating. The third situation that commonly lead couples to emotional disengagement is when one or both persons made a conscious choice to stop investing in their partner due to personality defect, mental health disorders, or for many years of hurt and frustration after trying. We will explore all of those in greater detail.

A person who is passive in their communication will struggle with tremendous anxiety when sharing their thoughts, feelings, or needs with a partner. They will ruminate and churn over, again and again before stating their position. They will imagine that their partner will react in an unpleasant way and respond with anger or irritation if they talk about a grievance. The pitfall here is that their partner is completely unaware that there is any problem. Imagine the scenario, Carl and his wife Jenny have been married for 15 years. After their second child was born, their sex life greatly diminished. At first, Carl tried to hold Jenny at night, and made attempts to be closer to her intimately. Each time, Jenny froze and shut down. Carl stopped trying and feared upsetting Jenny by discussing his sexual needs. He even started seeing a therapist to talk about his hurt and anger towards his partner, but at home, he never said a word. Jenny, for all of these years thought that their relationship was perfect and was more than a little shocked when she discovered that he had been seeing a therapist. He still refused to talk about what took him there. Without appropriate and necessary feedback, our partner plods along in an artificial world of imagined and perfect marital bliss. Feedback is vital lifeblood for the union and the survival of any relationship; thus, we must be courageous enough to provide it. It is similar to our workplace performance review: sharing is caring, and is an opportunity to grow closer together. If we care about our partner, we must share what makes us unhappy. We must also foster an awareness of the tremendous anxiety that undermines each partner's efforts to communicate needs. Here is the shocking truth, just like with Carl who feared his partners response, we create the distance that we fear making by the means we use to prevent it, a sort of self-fulfilling prophecy. Silence and avoidance are true a barriers to building a happy relationship.

Intimacy avoidance is harder to detect and develop insight around compared to other communication and relationship styles. This is characteristic of a partner who, like the passive communicator, also suffers tremendous anxiety about sharing, but their angst is deeply internal and takes place more on an unconscious level. In fact, this personality type may be unlikely to enter into a relationship at all. While avoidance exists on a spectrum with some who can tolerate some closeness, others defenses are so high that they can only let a partner enter their world in micro-doses before retreating. Intimacy avoidants keep their inner world tucked out of sight, searching for a reproach or a reason to remain quiet after taking any emotional risk. They offer a bit of themselves and then rapidly retreat from their fear of being judged, left, or criticized. Their terror of others causes a kind of deafening paralysis that they will struggle with for life without professional intervention. Yet even when these vulnerable persons do enter into a relationship, their partner often ends up feeling con-fused by the pushing and pulling of their alternating dance of com-ing closer and retreating. Then the avoidant's anxiety mounts, and even if it seems that things have been progressing wonderfully, they turn away. They baffle their partner who ends up feeling unlovable, frustrated, and unimportant. This personality type, because of their lack of insight into the mechanics of their motivations, may also be prone to projecting the blame for their inability to connect on their partner. They may in fact believe that they are responding to the lack of support, affection, or attention in the relationship. Mindfulness is harder to manifest here and will require both persons to exercise an awareness of sharing their true needs and to create an atmosphere of insight for their mutual desire to change the patterns. Empathy for the self as well as for both parties in the relationship is needed, yet difficult to attain.

The final way that lovers start to practice communication avoid-ance is that they make a conscious choice to stop moving toward each other. This is a frighteningly common scenario that couples end up in if they bottle up their frustration about past, unmet needs. They purposefully stop communicating, stop prioritizing their intimacy, and decide against consistently connecting with each other. Yet it is also easy to understand how this happens with such frequency in our modern world. For a counselor or a motivated couple, there is a pathway to change, to instead move toward reconnection. For instance, if over the years, our lover shows little interest in responding to us, we stop making overtures toward connecting. Maybe they work so much, or adopt the role of parent and leave behind their role as lover—a very human pattern of behavioral conditioning. If they do remain in the relationship, the lonely partner will instead create a life outside of the relationship. As a substitute they lean on their friends and persons who act as surrogates for our valid and universal human need for intimacy and connection. In this style of relationship, it is important to acknowledge and mourn the mutual hurt and anger caused by distance, while simultaneously and constructively providing the potential of hope for reconnection. It takes much bravery to choose hope when there have been years of deep chasm of distance. Imagine the couple Erin and Lynn: They have been in a domestic partnership for 6 years. When they moved to Nevada for Erin's work, Lynn was more than supportive. Yet, Erin's work as a veterinarian continued to be the focal point of her life. At first, Lynn tried to talk with Erin about it, but Lynn did not feel heard and the conversations did not result in change. Instead, over the years, it became a topic that immediately created a palpable fury between them, with Erin refuting, "What would we do without me working 80 hours a week? We would never be able to hold our investments or keep this home. Why don't you get a job to help!" Rough conversations indeed. Lynn stopped mentioning it. Instead she began to join her community golf club, the rotary club, meetup groups and became friends with many people in the community. It is healthy for people to have relationships outside of their primary relationship, but in this instance, the distance between Lynn and her partner was so deep and long standing that they didn't even know the other important people in their separate lives.

In closing this section, we take with us an understanding that verbal communication is the nest which contains the emotional, physical, and actual sentiments that form the vivid and taut fibers of our intimate relationship. Communication has great potential but entails a tremendous responsibility. This is because if practiced improperly, it presents many risks of cutting off connection and instead moving toward conflict and disconnection. By using the mechanisms of mindfulness, we are able to counter many of the potential pitfalls of communication and to bring it back to the direction of mutual and loving, supportive relatedness.

Becoming mindful in our relationship is not a singular task. Consistent commitment is required from both partners in order to adhere to the strategies of awareness, to become keenly aware of what we are feeling, and to then assess and strategize how our partner is responding, all the while managing our own feelings, thoughts, and needs. Our words should be aimed at soothing our partner, not magnifying our own position or accelerating our partner's hurt. Communication and management of our feelings is a necessary form of self-care aimed at fostering emotional awareness and relationship strength. This is without a doubt the creative force which contributes to the emotional and physical climate of our cherished romantic connection.

While it is easy to fix our gaze on the other person when we start a discussion about what is wrong in the relationship, or to peer outside of ourselves in discussing what changes should be made in the relationship, this approach is wrong. Always we must first examine ourselves, in proper Socratic Method, which means we commit to questioning everything. On our best days, we only have control over ourselves and the responses that we give to others. We have the best outcomes when we focus on how to better understand and shape our own behavior. Mindfulness is challenging work. When we are exercising it well, we become aware of things that make us uncomfortable and things that we do to sabotage our best efforts to love and be loved. Relationships are riddled with challenges and facing up to them takes work. Having a stable marriage or long term relationship with someone with whom we share a deep loving connection, one which offers support and understanding over the years of our lifetime is a beautiful goal and worth every effort that we must make in order to achieve it.

CHAPTER TEN

MINDFUL MAKE-UP: IF YOU WANT TO MAKE THINGS BETTER, LISTEN BEFORE YOU SPEAK

No matter how much progress we make in becoming mindful lovers and effective communicators, we will sometimes be unsuccessful in our attempts to forge understanding. Some of the disagreements may even turn into shouting matches, blow outs, or days of unwelcome and unpleasant silence. We all know the defeating experience of having an argument where both parties end up feeling dehumanized, hurt, and misunderstood. Becoming mindful of our relationship patterns requires us to learn the skill of repairing the conflict so that each person can be understood and have their needs acknowledged as valid and important. When we don't repair the damage that is done on the ragged path of hostile conflict, we erode the long term quality of our relationship. Partners and even whole families can end up being very disconnected from each other. Sometimes we sweep the tensions under the rug, which isn't always a bad tactic, but if we too frequently refrain from attempting to discuss the conflict again because our life's lessons have limited our understanding of the possibilities for communication, we lose out. Facing the grim prospect that things can go wrong, we imagine that any discussion will lead to further fights. We may end up travelling down the abyss of avoidance by way of fear of talking with our partner.

We must notice our behavior and try to find a new way of communicating and repairing conflict. In fact, for couples who enter therapy for help, teaching them how to process and move on from disagreements is often the second stage of their counseling formula.

The first thing that we should assess when becoming mindful of the communication in any relationship is which style of conflict resolution each partner typically enacts. There are many different styles of conflict resolution. Some of us need time to cool down after a disagreement, while others feel an urgent need to resolve a conflict immediately. If these two personalities form a relationship, their quarrels can turn into wars and their differences into a conflict of personalities. First, think about which one of you usually tries to repair a conflict first. How does each of you usually attempt to repair your disagreements? Pause, and think deeply about this. Many people say: *We don't repair, we don't talk about it, we just move on and don't bring it up again until next time we blow up about it.* This response indicates an area that we can offer detailed attention to the betterment of the relationship.

Another style is when one partner becomes very anxious and demands to iron it all out on the spot. The anxiety can become so great that it leads the partner into the erroneous belief that continued discussion will close the chasm both of you feel. When one partner has a style that demands closure while the other partner is attempting to retreat to take some space to calm down, if that space to self-soothe and process is not honored by the partner who has a need for immediate conflict resolution, the result is often chaos. For example, imagine Tara and Rob: They were in a relationship for 5 years when they entered therapy for the second time because their relationship started to feel even more dangerous and unpredictable. Tara tearfully described that she had been trying to use the conflict management plan when they had disagreements about how to parent their two small children. She sobbed saying she didn't understand what she was doing wrong, and that when she took space to self-soothe in their bedroom, Rob would come thundering in after her. He was often in a rage at this point and demanded that they talk it out right now. The more that he became angry, the more frightened she felt and the more desperately she tried to retreat, but this seemed to make it worse. Most recently, Rob broke through the bedroom, refusing to be "locked out of his own god damn house!" As a group, and Tara and I individually, talked about safety. Through many more meetings, we were able to process emotional management and different conflict resolution styles again. Rob was able to acknowledge the feeling of abandonment that emerges for him when Tara retreats to the bedroom and he was able to see the wisdom of having some time between the fight to try to talk about it. This illustrates well how the person who is not able to reach their desired need for closure feels increasingly overwhelmed and potentially angry and demanding of their needs being met. This kind of pairing can pose great challenges when trying to repair and reduce conflict. The final style is the couple who says they never disagree or argue. As mentioned in the previous chapter, in that kind of relationship, there is likely distance, coolness, and a dire need for much more honest communication.

Summarizing previous sections, no matter which style of conflict resolution one has, one can benefit by adopting a protocol for conflict management that works for you. Starting with a cooling off period of anywhere from thirty minutes to several hours can help us to be in our best problem-solving mode, instead of the activated and aroused state of fight or flight. Remember, we shouldn't scream our need for a cool off space at our partner. We should state our need to cool down gently, never glaring and wordlessly storming off. After letting our partner know that we need some time to calm down, we go to a quiet place and use some of our self-soothing strategies such as diversions or diaphragmatic breathing. These help us to calm down before re-engaging in the conflict discussion. When we are ready, we then use the following steps to repair mindfully.

Most people who unsuccessfully try to repair a disagreement falsely believe the following: *If my partner hears and understands what I am saying, then they will be able to make the right changes and the problem will be resolved.* This is only partly true. Most people are only able to listen well after feeling completely understood. Helping our partner *to be* understood instead of forcing them to understand is a novel approach to reach mutual understanding, but a highly effective one. We extend the olive branch and apply the healing salve of curious empathy toward our beloved sees things. Mindfully repairing conflict requires a four-step process and mounds of emotional control and wisdom. The most important time to apply these lessons is when it will be most difficult, for example when we are absolutely infuriated by what our partner is explaining. It is especially true that when we sign on for a relationship, we prioritize being caring and compassionate as opposed to winning or always being right. If our relationship is to be a healthy and nurturing one, we are obliged to maintain our calm, reflective dignity and listen to our partner's point of view, trying to glean the pearls of agreement between us.

Step one is to approach our beloved with genuine curiosity and ask them to share their perspective. We might start by saying some of the following statements:

"I am really sorry that things have gotten out of hand; I want to understand your perspective on this topic more deeply."

"I think there are certain things I may have missed about your thoughts and feelings on this; can you share a little more?"

"I know our last attempt at discussing this didn't end well, but I am calmer now and would like to try again; let me know when you are ready."

Even if we have had the same disagreement five hundred times, give it your best to use this format. Then listen, truly, genuinely listen and provide your partner with the chance to share. Don't interrupt or insert your opinion or tell them why everything they are saying is wrong. Refrain from inserting 'yes,' or 'but.' Lavish the nourishing salve of attention and focused appreciation on your beloved without trying to change anything about what they think and feel.

We can compare this attitude of quiet observation with the way that we observe our feelings and thoughts when doing our mindfulness meditation. The hallmark of mindful practice is adhering to the practice of non-judgment of our thoughts, feelings, and internal observations. We do the same exercise with our partner. This will also require us to do some deep breathing and to continue soothing ourselves during their explanation, as most likely we will not agree with their interpretation of things. We don't need to agree completely or experience bliss at each utterance that we are hearing, but we do need to maintain emotional control over ourselves so that we can listen in a way that provides attention and respect. Be especially aware of non-verbal expressions. I have observed many couples who master the art of listening deliberately but have murderous non-verbals. Remember if you are muttering, speaking in harsh tones or name-calling, you are not in a space to resolve anything. While we may say one thing, we are indicating hostile disagreement by glaring or scowling, which then increases the likelihood that our partner will shut down because they are feeling judged and threatened. Non-verbal communication is one part content, one part tone, and one part non-verbal facial and physical expressions. We should aim at active listening which requires making direct eye contact, nodding to encourage more feedback, and maintaining body posture facing our partner or spouse.

Step two: Ask and Ask A Lot. Ask as many questions as you can, questions that are aimed at understanding their feelings, thoughts, and needs. It takes mindfulness and insight to move away from the potential pitfalls of this step of repairing the conflict. The normal tendency is to ask questions that are aimed at solving the problem such as, 'how can we do this differently' or to ask defensive questions such as 'how can you really think this the case?' Or, the receiver produces questions that attempt to minimize their partner's position, or to dominate the conversation by sharing their own perspective, thus frustrating the speaker and stunting their effort to create understanding. There are a million ways to get understanding wrong. For every failed communication attempt that has been unraveled on my therapy couch, without delay or deviation, any attempt to counter a partner emphatically explaining a problem with the phrase, 'you're wrong that's not what I meant!' always creates bigger problems. When we tell our partner that we wish there was more sexual intimacy in the relationship, and they respond with 'we have sex four times a month; that's more than many,' we have minimized our partners' feelings and perspective. They will only become more frustrated.

The antidote is to intensify our mindfulness, to instead hone in on what our partner is feeling. We can only do this by asking about their feelings. Some starter questions are

"How did you feel when_____?"

"When else do you feel this way?"

"What is most hurtful or frustrating about this for you?"

As you may notice, we are exhibiting openness and understanding when we ask these questions without making any effort to change or alter our partner's emotional and cognitive assessment of what is happening. This is a truly mindful moment. By being actively curious about our partner's feelings, we embody the wisdom of the sage. There is a fantastic metaphor in Indian philosophy: *To be like the lotus which sits in the water but does not get wet.* We do not need to react to the angst of others. We should try to understand and soothe other's hurts. Yet the truth is, the majority of people do walk around becoming upset when told by others that they are being irritated or hurt by them, exemplifying the old adage, adding insult to injury. Nevertheless, with practice, it is possible to sit in the mud gently anchored on our roots, floating peacefully. Most of the time, other people's reactions have little to do with us. Even when we do our best to meet our partners and friends with acceptance of their feelings, they will provoke something in us, from compassion and empathy to aggression. As an act of mindfulness, we should be aware of the physical sensations in our own body when we are listening, but only to make a mental note of them. Our primary focus remains moving close to our lover by cradling and nurturing their emotional perspective.

Step three: Acknowledge that you have taken it all in. We are most likely to accept the perspective of a person who has first taken the time to understand our own perspective. Reflect understanding by giving your best effort at summarizing what you have heard. Start by saying:

"So, I really want to get this right, tell me if I understand you correctly, because of _____ (Fill this in with step one), you feel _____." (Fill this in with step two).

This script allows us to share compassionate understanding and empathy, and has tremendous nourishing effects on our relationship. When we can seek to empathize with our spouses' feelings even when they have a different experience or understanding from our own, our love bond is strengthened. It is not synchronicity of thought and preference that strengthens the fabric of our marriage, it is the effort and miracle of compassion that creates well bonded connections.

The fourth step is to offer understanding or validation. We can use the following template in offering our understanding:

"It makes sense that you feel _____ because of _____."

Remember this doesn't mean that you agree with your partner's position; you are just understanding it. Understanding and agreement are two very different things. It's never up to us to change the way another person thinks or feels. It's ok if our partner is irritated or unhappy in this moment. It must also be ok for each of you to have different perspectives. We aren't seeking to make an agreement of unison. Our only goal is repairing to make peace by understanding each other more.

We become more and more mindful of some universal truths about communication. When things do get out of hand, emotions run hot, and words that are spoken cannot ever be slithered back into our mouths. What we do have, if we are lucky, is more time to keep living our lives, time to try to do better in nourishing our love and a chance of offering better listening and speaking next time. We have opportunities to learn and change. Try to learn from your previous disagreements. We can improve our method of communication with all of the lessons that our previous missteps provide. The next time you find yourself in conflict, use it as an example and opportunity to raise the bar of your efforts in forging a pathway to healthy communication that ensures the future of your marriage or romantic relationship.

Compromise

If you are like many people, you may be sort of frustrated or disappointed about the previous sections. Their lesson is that we must make our goal one of service and giving our attention and understanding. Your ego may be wondering, *Hey, what about me?* That change is made when we leave behind the notion that our perspective must be shared at all times and the immature expectation that our partner bend to our needs. Love and communication must first be all about the other. The real goal is for both partners to enter collaboration mode and become mindful of their lover, their emotional selves, and to move toward understanding and gratitude instead of hyper-focusing on the perceived inadequacies of their partners.

If we are perfectly honest with ourselves, we should admit that simply by the mechanisms of our own humanness, we are undeniably selfish creatures and full of craving. Human craving and endless desire are some of the core tenets of Buddhism. We are always aware of our own impulses and needs. We say, *How can she think that I don't pay attention? I always pay attention; she is so selfish!* We give in to our wish for ten more minutes of the fishing excursion, expecting others to go along with our demands, and we become discouraged when they inevitably don't. We also may think, *I deserve this time, attention, sympathy, encouragement.* Yet, this isn't the nature of love; love reaches beyond the self to offer care for the other. One of the cornerstones of any relationship is compromise. We must let go of our own ego in order to hear and cradle the essence of our partner. We must give up our want for unlimited time and attention, for mounds of sex, for constant reassurance. Instead, we should nurture our relationship and connect by giving. Giving also has its caveats. Proper giving means giving what our partner wants and not what we want to give. Read that previous line again please! Even when our partner wants something that we are not willing or able to give, it is ok. Why? Because in that moment, we can still give understanding, attention, and thought. If we are in a relationship, we must always pause to give that.

We achieve compromise best by cultivating our ability to have mental and emotional flexibility; we must bend. Couples do create conflict for themselves when they refuse to bend or are rigidly immobile in their childish defenses of oppositional defiance, for example when someone is prone to reject their partner's every request for understanding, (the 'yes, but' or the flat out 'no'). We can note that a 'yes, but' partner is locked in the teenage stage of rebelling. They cannot allow their partner inside the sphere of influence or to access their inner vulnerability. They still cling to rejecting a component of their partner's perspective. Healthy relationships thrive on collaboration and the ability to both accept and at times mold each other. Without allowing our partner to shape our behavior, we become like two cement pillars standing side by side, strong and erect, but never touching. The truth is even in the best relationships, there will be differences in attitude, likes and interests that involve compromise.

The Yes and No Game: Coming toward the middle takes practice. A helpful exercise for understanding the shape of your interactional patterns is playing the Yes and No Game. This is a communication exercise where we mock agreement. It will also serve to illuminate our communication style. Sit with your partner cross legged and face to face. Each of you gets the chance to talk about five topics that may or may not have something to do with the relationship. My recommendation is that you begin by talking for a minute about something that is going on in your life and is outside of the relationship. As we previously learned, it is more difficult to approach topics that involve the relationship. It may be a topic that is irritating, or a problem you are working on solving, even something that was recently disappointing.

The partner who is listening provides no feedback but instead nods in agreement and says,

"Yes I can understand why you feel _____."

That's it, nothing more. Just stick with the template here, even if and especially if it feels unnatural to not add in anything more. It will be easier to agree with the first two statements if they are about work or a situation related to someone in the family. Try this again, search for something else that happened and share it in great detail and the listener repeats the above line.

For the listener, make note of how hard it was to speak in agreement. Are you learning that your natural tendency is to be in agreement or disagreement most often? Many people err on one side or the other most easily.

For the next step, now that you have both warmed up a bit, the speaker then talks about something within the relationship. The speaker will share their own feelings and not talk about their partner, for example, "I feel _____ about, _____." Each person should speak only about their own feelings and avoid the tendency to blame anyone else for the problem. Just state what you feel.

The listener now practices mindfulness by noting what they feel in their body, what emotions arise. Just make a mental note here, but respond with head nodding and an affirmative—

"Yes, I can understand why you feel _____."

This is a very important step in the sequence. If we notice internal irritation, anger or disbelief, we must not project that toward our partner. Do you want to disagree or respond with your own thoughts? Take note of what is going on within you and work toward openness. Or, perhaps you nodded in agreement to everything but ended up feeling like a puppet, yearning to have the courage to challenge your partner at times? Use what you have learnt about practicing patience and openness, still caring about your partner even when their beliefs or points of view are different from our own.

Then each person takes turns and the roles are switched.

This exercise fosters awareness of our natural tendency to hinder our partner from entering our sphere of understanding. The more difficult this is, the more it reveals our innate defensiveness and tendency to reject our partner's needs. Try to remain non-judgmental of yourself too, even as you notice how challenging it is for you to achieve this state of understanding and accepting. We easily avoid a rut of misunderstanding when we let go of the goal of challenging and accepting. This can sometimes be characteristic of certain personality profiles that exhibit a high level of defensiveness, difficulty in accepting persuasion from others, and a higher need for control. It may take much practice to restrain our irritation while role playing in the 'yes game,' but allow your emotional response to signal a heightened awareness about your own innate tendencies. The more irritating and unnatural if feels to nod in agreement with your partner's thoughts, the more likely that you are starving your partner from receiving validation, understanding, and compromise.

When we love someone, we don't get to pick and choose when we will participate in loving them. If we withhold affection and warmth because our partner doesn't comply with our way of seeing issues the way we want them to, we are depriving everyone involved of a healthy, loving atmosphere. Accepting the responsibility of love means we are still required to give them love and compassion. If we withhold affection, understanding and connection unless they think and feel our way, then we are not really participating in a relationship. We are actually just passing time and sharing superficial fun without providing true loving care. To love, even when it is hard, this is what it means to be married or to share in a relationship.

Now that you have adequately understood your partner and your own defense style, it is time to form a strategy for compromise. Below are some more questions to ask that will move you and your partner toward compromise. In an ideal world, we would always get to speak our minds and have our partner hear us and potentially even agree with our thoughts, but this isn't practical. You will need a tool to use when you have disagreements that touch on things that are very important to both of you. For this part, each partner should make a list of two columns. One is made up of problematic topics you can compromise on, the other being areas within these topics that you will not be flexible on. These are your core needs or boundaries.

After writing these lists, trade them and talk about it while *not* trying to solve the problems. Just try to understand your partner's areas of inflexibility, but to do it in a way that allows you to understand what is very important about these areas of inflexibility. Be sure to use questions like,

"Where do you boundaries lay with this topic?"

"In which parts of this situation do you feel unwilling to change?"

"Are there any parts to this that you do feel a bit more flexible about?"

"How can I be sensitive of your needs while maneuvering around your boundaries?"

Then, as always, switch roles to create a mutual and two-sided dialogue.

Although moving toward compromise is a tool for achieving a mindful relationship, we must also balance this with a measure of healthy boundaries. To compromise doesn't mean that we allow our partner to take over deciding everything for us, but that we know when to yield and when to stand up. Most individuals have a deficit in either yielding or setting boundaries. Pay attention to whether it is more difficult to say yes or no for you. If saying yes comes with natural ease, then saying no might be the place to practice more mindfulness. When it comes to matters of safety, honesty, and vitally important boundaries, we cannot ever compromise on those. Moreover, those who love us should also want to respect and honor those needs. Do the following exercise to assess how well your relationship is incorporating boundary crossings and compromises, as well as your communication about them.

1) Get a paper and draw three columns.

2) Make a list of 10 boundaries in the first column. Think deeply about this. If it is hard for you to come up with them, you may also imagine calling them deal breakers.

3) In the second column, write a check mark next to any boundaries that this relationship has ever stepped over.

4) Make a third column that is associated with the second column. Here we will put a check mark next to it for any time that a boundary was crossed, and your partner attempted to have one or multiple processing conversations about what went wrong after the boundary crossing event. Note if you or your partner did his or her best to apologize, to acknowledge and validate

what was felt, and whether they made assurances that these same behaviors wouldn't be repeated.

5) To rate your relationship's performance, take note: If you are noticing lots of boundary crossings and few checks in the processing column, it is likely that you or your partner are not being honest about needs and/or feelings. You have probably pent up frustrations that could be worked through to create greater understanding, opportunities for compromise, and a stronger, loving connection.

CHAPTER ELEVEN

BEING ACCOUNTABLE AND RESPONSIBLE

Accountability is a potential treasure trove of harmonizing abundance for couples who want to learn the art of preventing and recovering from disagreements. Accountability starts internally. In the words of Socrates, *know thyself.* It is not easy work to know the motivations, meanings, and outcomes of the things that we say and do. The quest for truth and self-understanding takes many people to therapists' offices. The difficulty is further compounded by the challenge faced by the reality that humans beings are unreliable narrators of our own actions. When our partner says, "you seem upset," the reflex toward denial and minimization instantly kicks in: "I am NOT upset" we often reply in an elevated tone of voice.

When we are not accountable or honest with ourselves and our partner, we dam up the flow of truth and connection, creating an emotional atmosphere of impenetrable stagnation. Have you ever seen a river bed that was narrow and full of rocks and logs preventing water from passing through? That is like the blocked energy of honesty in the relationship. Being unaccountable, either on purpose or inadvertently, will lead to many battles and heated disagreements. Lying on purpose or failing to be accountable for what we have done is called gaslighting.

Gaslighting is a term derived from the 1944 movie titled "Gaslight," where the main character is systematically led to believe that she is mentally unwell and hallucinating her partner's poor behavior. Let us imagine an example illustrated by Kim and Jake: Kim has been noticing that Jake has been drinking much more than usual recently. This is alarming to Kim because she and Jake met in recovery and had vowed to not slip back into those same behaviors. Jake is adamantly denying everything, yet Kim has even found empty beer cans in the garage and she has noticed that Jake has been sneaking outside with increasing frequency. Kim is very anxious to mention it, fearing that it will lead to a blow-up. She is beside herself when she shares this situation in the individual portion of their couples therapy session. Kim was told about the importance of talking about the issue together in their couples session and for forming a plan to see how therapy could help.

However, when she attempted to discuss it with her partner, Jake replied, "Beer cans in the garage? Are you crazy? Those must have been there from before we moved in! I am not sneaking out and drinking beer. I have been trying to help you by walking the dog more! I swear, you are always accusing me of something, I can't take this anymore." Then he stormed off, leaving the session. In that moment, with denial and defensiveness, Jake did not exhibit any accountability. Kim ended up feeling bad about herself for even mentioning the beer cans. She even described wondering if maybe she had been imagining it or had missed those beer cans in the garage when she cleaned out the garage months ago. This is how gaslighting works. As times goes on, if gaslighting continues to happen, she will keep bringing up the excessive drinking and the mounting evidence, raising her voice louder and more frequently in order to be heard, but without accountability, there will be no change. She will eventually feel more and more frustrated and confused.

Imaging how different that session would have gone if instead, when Kim mentioned the beer cans, Jake had said, "I am really glad you're bringing this up. I've been struggling lately and didn't know how to tell you that I started drinking. I feel so ashamed of myself."

With such accountability and vulnerability, if Kim is practicing self-awareness and compassion, she will likely be pulled to help her partner and provide him some support. As a side note, discussion and understanding are vital. It is also true that we all deserve to know the truth. Trying to manage this is vital. It is worth noting that there are some differences when the presenting issue is addiction and alcohol or drug abuse. There is little we can do to force others into recovery, particularly when there is no accountability or desire to change. Yet, denial is the defensive hallmark of addiction. Confusion, anger, hurt and disagreement follow when we fail to expose vulnerable truths and become responsible for ourselves.

Denial is the ally of low levels of accountability. Of course, not every disagreement or situation that has to do with unaccountability in a relationship is related to addiction. There are lots of other embarrassing or uncomfortable situations which are hard for us to admit to ourselves or to others. It can be about household issues like parenting, cleaning, or paying the bills. The gamut of issues we encounter can be the springboard for defensiveness that happens when our partner brings up a point that is hard for us to admit. To nurture our accountability, we first of all need to become very honest with ourselves so that we are able to consider accurately what is happening around us and *because* of us.

Validation is a very different from accountability. Accountability says, "I own my faults." However, I tell the couples who trust me with their care that to learn to give validation is the single most important tool that they can take away from counseling. It can reduce conflict, calm a person rather quickly, and like a voodoo doll, ward off bad vibes! Validation, no matter the issue, is like saying, *Yes, I understand what you are saying and your world makes sense to me!* How calming is that in the heat of an argument? We really need a lot of validation coursing through our love to keep it healthy.

There is much literature about the psychologically damaging effects of the invalidation relationship between partners, as well as between the parent and child. Invalidation literally is a founding cause of things like personality disorders. Validation has been shown to reduce the likelihood that a trauma survivor will develop PTSD. You might wonder why we started the validation section with accountability, and there is a reason: We must be accountable if we are going to validate the other people in our life. Let's check in on your relationship and get some honesty about what is happening between you and your partner. As you become hyper-aware, you can practice the exercise below to further become more accountable to those around you. Be patient with yourself; this will require some practice.

Get out your paper and let's make another list. Record what happened the last several times your partner tried to discuss something upsetting to them with you, maybe coming home late, taking all of the covers in bed, forgetting to pick up milk on your way home. Now, just think about it. How did you respond?

Write an A next to the time that you agreed,

B next to the times you became defensive or minimized their concern,

C next to the times that you became hostile and yelled at them for their perception.

If you validated that their concern did in fact happen, how did that conversation turn out? Did your partner calm down with the effect of being understood?

Or, if you marked B and you closed up like a clam, shutting out your partner's reasoning, how did that conversation turn out? Did you tell them something along the lines of "I don't know what you're talking about?" or, "How can you be saying this, don't you remember all of the times I did _____?" Did your partner become even more upset and hostile? When we become defensive and we deflect, or when we minimize what happened, we miss valuable opportunities for learning, and nothing gets understood.

Countering our tendency to minimize our partner's concerns and to defend ourselves is to instead respond by validating our partner when they raise a point of accountability. Do not wave your hand dismissively finding the points where their statement isn't true.

Instead, think about how what is said could be true. Even if you have to burrow down and hunt for the little kernel of shared reality within what was proffered, when you are looking for it, you will find it. Or, you should be able to find something there that is true for them, unless of course our partner really is a deceptive sociopath, a pathological liar, or is suffering psychosis. In that case, none of the teachings in this text will apply. This book is intended for the many average people who are reasonably good, fair, and lucid. Instead of pushing away the truth to defend ourselves, the goal is to teach ourselves to be vulnerable, accountable, and validating to ourselves and to our partner. The more we acknowledge our mistakes, the more those around us will be inspired to also respond with accountability. Here we make the active choice to create a culture of honesty, transparency, and hopefulness.

CHAPTER TWELVE

FORGIVENESS

Any person who seeks to enter a relationship and remain it for more than a few months at a time had better enhance their capacity for forgiveness. Forgiveness becomes a regular action in a long-term marriage. By our imperfect nature, we sometimes forget, we do things that are thoughtless, we can be short tempered and over-zealous. There is no perfect love or relationship. What we do have are people who attempt to do their best and to practice forgiveness with each other and themselves when they fall short of their best intentions. A love without forgiveness is a minefield of suffering. We become strained and immobile in that sort of relationship when we are unable to give or receive forgiveness. We become unable to move toward connection for fear of stepping into the harsh and unforgiving terrain. Imagine what would ensue if trees tried to grow each spring covered in the mottled and dead leaves of the previous autumn's shedding. Instead, each year, they grow faint as nature's mechanisms prevail on autumn's progress. The leaves turn to dry and crumbled rust before melding into the darkness of winter, using their death only to nourish the earth around it. Our nature must be like that of the tree, not clinging to past disappointments and misgivings but letting those fall to the earth, finding the wisdom from each failure and empowering our love from the lessons learned. Letting go of hurt means that we talk together about what has happened, shedding the leaves, and then we use our empathy and thoughtfulness to find understanding.

Letting go of hurt means that we take the time to talk about what has happened. We shed the leaves as we process the disagreements by using validation, empathy and accountability to solve our problems. We use empathetic communication to create understanding and insight about what went wrong, nourishing the roots of our relationship, and we each do our part to assure that we will act differently in the future.

Most of the time, we will find that we hold completely different perspectives about what happened that led to the disagreement, or come to a different understandings of how the conflict should have been handled. In such instances, we may not be able to move toward a common standpoint, or we may not find a pathway towards agreement about making a behavior change. Our goal may simply be to talk about it and try to understand our partner's perspective. What this means exactly is that when we are in love or married, we must be capable of letting go, forgiving our partner for things that they don't even believe that they did wrong. This can be hard to do. In some instances, we may be called upon to forgive each other more than once each and every day. The more we open our eyes to the wisdom of cultivating mindfulness in our relationship, we see that managing a change in a relationship is not for the weak or faint of heart.

In order to truly forgive, we don't mention the disagreement to provoke shame or guilt in our partner at every chance that we get. We put it aside. We bury it and we commit to not pulling this evidence of our partners' fallibility or imperfection into any more conversations after we have processed its meaning to both partners. This is in direct opposition to the pain caused by holding on to hurt. There is a wise proverb which states that holding a grudge is like drinking poison and expecting the other person to die. Grudges don't cause harm to anyone other than ourselves. The Dalai Lama says that we do not forgive for the other person; we forgive for ourselves. Our whole marriage or relationship can become bitter when we remember more vividly the things that our partner has not done or done wrong, rather than reflect on the memory of the way that they affect our lives positively. When our way of perceiving our love is masked in complete disappointment, our whole perception of our once cherished love changes. Then we will notice that even our lover's good deeds are effaced by the corrosion of disappointment and anger.

This is a symptom of a very troubled relationship. This section of the text does not say that we must forgive everything all of the time. There may be things that have happened between the two of you which were unbearable deal breakers. Yet, this isn't a book on breaking up or how to determine whether a relationship has become unsalvageable. This is a book about maintaining and nourishing a loving relationship. In that way, regular cleansing of our memories and letting go of hurt is a part of what keeps our love vital and healthy.

Here is another mindful exercise we should use to help us let go of our anger and hurt. You may notice that most of these exercises begin with breathing. We do not offer this out of repetition but out of necessity.

Take a seat in your favorite comfortable space, sit down and find your breath.

Begin by taking long, slow, deep diaphragmatic breaths.

Let go of the present and get deep into your breathing.

Now do some visualization: Imagine your partner as you think about whatever things have happened between the two of you. Think of their face, and consider it deeply.

Now assess how you feel in this moment as you think about what events are unfolding between the two of you.

Label your emotions and offer yourself compassion and understanding for what you feel.

Breathe in a bright white light, and breathe out while aiming the loving light toward the person or partner with whom you have disagreed.

Imagine on inhalation that the white light is filling you both each time you breathe in. Each time you breathe out, the white love disperses around you both.

Allow your partner to be bathed in understanding, compassion, belief in their goodness.

Notice where in your body your feel tightness or holding on as you think of the hurts you carry in your heart.

Do this for around ten minutes and then use your journal afterwards to further process what this felt like for you. Prompt yourself to consider what you felt like immediately after the exercise was over and also what was difficult about doing it. It's an eternal truth that the act of forgiveness takes time. Use your journal to produce an inner dialogue which focuses on *what you imagine it will feel like when you do forgive completely*. Also, focus on what will change in the way that you interact with each other in the relationship. Be very thorough as you write about this. Remember to be patient and calm in allowing your thoughts to come gently and at their own pace. Do not rush yourself through, but rather, be aware and deliberate in your process.

CHAPTER THIRTEEN

TRUST

We all know that trust is a foundational and vital component of every relationship, yet we find that many people still have to learn what trust means. Think about it, what comes to your mind when you consider trust? Pause and think of the answer to the question: *Do you trust your partner?* Be very honest with yourself here. If you struggle to trust your partner due to something that has happened in the relationship, then working to repair it with them, on your own or with a therapist should be a high priority. None of the other parts of the relationship can be nourished without this part. If you struggle to trust your partner but have no tangible reason not to, then perhaps trust is a struggle for you in all areas of life. We will examine what the full definition of trust is and how that plays into all of the parts of our bond. This includes trust in the commitment, trust in safety, and trust that our partner will treasure our secrets safely.

To trust is to have a belief in the reliability, truth, and ability of another person. We create trust by being reliably honest and consistent with each other over a long period of time. Trust is an unshakeable anchor upon which we can gladly place our faithfulness, optimism, and carve out our life plans without any qualms. To truly have that kind of base for our relationship, we are glad to give our honor and time, as we believe that our partner is more than worthy and will respond to us the same. To be trusted, we must act, speak and be in accordance with trusting behavior, and our partner should also be capable of recognizing and affirming us as trustworthy persons. They should acknowledge their belief in us. Trust goes both ways; *Does your partner trust you?* When was the last time in your life someone really believed in you, maybe a friend, co-worker, parent, or grandparent? To be a person who is believed in, to be a person lavished in trust builds us up; it gives us wings to fly. Consider the gift you are given when someone offers you their trust.

Conversely, to be distrusted is deflating, hurtful, and gravely frustrating, particularly when we are doing our best to be a good partner. When we look at the opposite of trust—mistrust, jealousy, and suspicion, we should first acknowledge that there is a baseline level of jealousy and suspicion that is normal. For example, you might feel a little jealous when your partner is talking to a pretty woman at the cocktail party. For those who are in the normal range in their feeling of jealousy, they may gently share it with their partner when they are driving home from the party. A healthy way of sharing might be a simple sentence without anger: "I felt so nervous and afraid (or angry/jealous) when you were talking to _____." If our partner is practicing mindfulness in the relationship, they will soothe our fear. After soothing and reassuring, maybe later you will both laugh it off or talk about how much you each love one another.

Those who struggle with expressing themselves will not convey their fear in a constructive way though. Instead of expressing the legitimate fear that they felt when observing their partner talking to the pretty woman at the cocktail party, they will express hostility or control. They may become damning, critical, angry with suspicions and accusations. This type of lack of trust comes from within and no amount of soothing by one's partner, no amount of behavior modification or limiting conversations at the cocktail party will allay this. It really must be fixed within. At the same time, the relationship can begin to tolerate some jealousy when partners use mindfulness to express it in a calm, vulnerable, and constructive way.

Having trust reaches into most facets of our relationship, from the emotional and physical to its potential for longevity. It keeps us emotionally safe and means many different things. Let us examine some of them as well as their obstacles before looking at a trust building exercise. Most people when asked to think about whether they trust their partner respond that they believe their partner is honest and upholds the agreed upon commitment of their relationship. If you and your partner agree to have a monogamous relationship, and believe that both of you are maintaining that commitment, this contributes to trust. It is also quite true that if there has been an infidelity in the relationship, trust will be scarce or impossible. When I am providing therapy to couples, I always note that attempting trust, is contraindicated for the relationship immediately after an affair. It may take years to rebuild any semblance of trust after an emotionally annihilating infidelity. For the person who has discovered the affair or been notified of an affair, there is often physical and emotional effects which closely mimic the symptoms of PTSD. The counseling interventions that work best in treating a relationship after an affair has been cut off should be focused on processing emotions such as hurt, and then working to rebuild trust and strengthening the various systems of the relationship after the processing has occurred.

In other cases, even if there has not been an affair, we may still struggle to build trust. Certain personality types will naturally have difficulties build trust. In the beginning stages, most relationships navigate through trust building. New relationships must assess whether the commitment is deepening to the point that would merit the effort of placing more trust in it.

Let us consider another form of trust, trust for physical safety. Do you feel physically and emotionally safe in your relationship? Can you trust that your partner will respect your right to physical distance and not harm your body? There is trust in that too. If there has been domestic violence in your relationship, then trusting your safety is going to be very hard. Unless the perpetrator of that violence has sought help for his or her anger and their dangerous expression of it, there is not much hope that trust in safety can exist. Yet it is also true that denial is one of the defense mechanisms which shore up the victim's ability to remain in the relationship as the domestic violence continues. Yet, violence doesn't always come in the form of physical threat. We can be violent with our words. When wanting to discuss a situation, things can get out of hand and become violent verbally or emotionally.

Still there is even more to the idea of trust. Can we trust that our partner will not leave us? Do we trust in their ability to maintain the commitment of the relationship by standing by our side for the duration of our lives together? Some barriers to maintaining this kind of trust exist when there has been a separation or threat of separation. In fact, some people hold the relationship hostage, as they say, by threatening to break up or actually breaking up with repetition frequency. In some kinds of unhealthy relationship patterns, one or both partners threaten to leave or breakup to prevent their partner from taking a stand or voicing opposition. It is particularly disabling when we have this sort of bedrock trust that the course of our relationship will continue on forevermore with our person by our side, only to learn that they want to end the relationship. Some would suggest that it is the rupture of this trust that makes such news most difficult. Of course, this creates fear, the opposite of love, and it is not possible to repair trust in the durability of such a relationship when repeated overtures indicate otherwise. There is a proverb which states, 'A king can control a country's action with fear, but not its heart.' The meaning is that we can sometimes control others through such actions, but we cannot make them continue to love us when we hold the relationship hostage.

The final kind of trust that we will cover is that which exists when we know that we can share our most hidden secrets, and we believe that our partner will keep them safe. When sharing some vulnerable information, maybe about something embarrassing that happened in the past, we give that morsel of open hurt to our partner. We trust that they will guard the treasure of our deepest vulnerabilities by holding it close and never revealing them to others. We must also be able to trust that our partner isn't going to use the tender bits of our past shames and disappointments against us in a disagreement in order to deliberately hurt us further. This is also trust.

Trust adds a layer of integrity and becomes a nucleus around which the other components of the relationship can crystallize and build. All of the above, the physical and emotional factors, commitment and honesty, build upon the emotional climate incubated in continually deepening our relationships.

The emotional ramifications of sustaining a trust- deficient relationship are anxiety, fear, and even panic. The benefits of nourishing love in a trusting environment are emotional warmth, stability, depth, and care. The truth is, there will be situations which come up that erode at our trust. Depending on the degree to which the person who lacks trust has mindfulness or insight into their deficiency, dire consequences can be mitigated. For example, when a partner with high self-insight notices their partner coming home thirty minutes late, the distrusting partner may say, "I know it's irrational, but I feel so anxious when you come home late. Is there anything going on that I should know about?" Here, the consequences are few because the high insight allows him or her to reach for their partner in a healthy way for soothing. A partner who has low insight into their lack of trust will often manifest blame toward their partner. This is called projection. They imagine their jealousy to be the responsibility of those around them and can also have aggressive reactions and lapse into fits and rages over situations which evoke a lack of trust. Using the same example above, a partner with low insight might say, "Where have you been? What is wrong with you? Tell me right now who you have been with!" If the other partner responds by trying to explain a traffic jam, this will not quell the suspicions. The distrusting partner will continue to rage and demand explanations.

To summarize, the level of mindful insight into our own inner deficit of trust has a direct effect on our ability to take ownership of our emotions, and will prevent us from blaming others or demanding that our partner make changes to manage our overabundance of angry jealousy. With low insight, we may blame our partner. With high insight, we acknowledge that we are struggling to trust, and we can then form an interaction that may be more constructive. When we are not conscious of our anxiety, we may seek to exert greater control over what's happening around us. We ask our partner to show us their phone, their email, to prove that they were where they say they were. We ask them not to spend time with friends without us present. The person who is in a relationship with one who struggles with trust may either exhibit defiance or they may start to limit their behavior to accommodate the irrational jealousy. Other reactions to lack of trust can be anger or frustration. These are normal and should be worked through with the help of a marriage counselor. In other situations where there hasn't been any cataclysmic trust shattering situation in the relationship, trust should be the focal point of our efforts in enhancing the relationship. As a couple, you may try some of the following exercises to build trust.

This is a physical exercise: The trust fall is a well known exercise because it offers a way to make the experience of trust tangible! We will try is here and then discuss the experience. Begin by locating a large open space that is free of debris and clutter. Read the instructions completely before beginning.

Both you and your partner will begin by standing about three feet apart, one behind the other and facing the same direction. The person who is standing in front will close his or her eyes and fall slowly backwards, letting him or herself go completely, trusting that their partner will catch them before they fall. The partner who is behind does their best to manage this trusting opportunity well by catching their beloved. Do it again, and ask each other how it felt. Be honest. Most people admit that it is scary and difficult to let go completely. How is it to catch? Now switch positions. It gives a whole new perspective on having each other's backs. The metaphor runs deep. Think about how each of you relates to the act of letting go and falling.

Do you trust your partner's strength and commitment to catch you?

What other thoughts and feelings come up during the exercise?

What was easiest about this?

What was hardest?

Be open to hearing the answers and lower your emotional defenses when receiving this information. It is when we share our truth and receive non-judgement, we start to trust.

Remember with all of the exercises to create a distraction free zone by turning all cell-phones, technology and media off or kept out of sight. This is sacred time in which we seal our intention and attune to our partner. It is important to quiet our minds of all unnecessary clutter and prepare to allow ourselves the benefit of showing our vulnerability and honesty. We will be uncovering layers of feeling.

This is a verbal exercise: Find a seat across from each other. This exercise works by enabling trust entrance into the deepest layers of the emotional spectrum, including sharing shame and fear. You and your partner will take turns communicating, playing the roles of both Sharing and Caring. The first person to Share responds to the question and The Caring Partner focuses on active listening without judgement. The caring partner asks each of the questions below in response to the Sharing. They do not criticize; they respond by offering only empathetic responses of care, love, and respect no matter what is shared. Go through the following questions together and remember to be gentle with each other. We build trust when we allow someone to know what is personal. Our feelings are some of the most personal expressions of ourselves. We then run the risk of allowing ourselves to be open to the vague possibility of being emotionally hurt. We often hide things about ourselves for fear of judgement, abandonment or ridicule, but when we open ourselves and unveil our inner layers, this is a chance for our partner to provide us with love, care, safety, interest, and tenderness. This exercise creates an atmosphere of emotional trust that strengthens our relationships.

Sharing Questions

What is something that you would like to change about yourself?

What is something embarrassing that has happened to you? You must come up with something.

What about your body or personality don't you like?

What has been your biggest perceived failure in life?

What part of your past are you most ashamed of?

Is there anything that you have done that you have felt guilty about?

What are you fears about the future?

The person who is in the Caring role will respond to each of the above questions by watching the facial expression of their partner to try to feel what their partner is feeling along with them. Then ask each of these questions in response to deepen the connection and conversation.

Caring Questions

How does this make you feel?

What is/was the hardest part about it?

When do you feel the effects of this?

Do you still struggle because of this?

Am I making you feel safe and loved right now?

Thank you for trusting me.

Now process this exercise. What has been hard about doing it? How did it feel? Is this similar to or different from how you normally share? Do you think you hold back sometimes in this relationship?

The goal of doing all of these exercises is to develop these skills so that this method of responding to each other becomes reflexive and normal. Trust, validation, emotional support, all of these are skills to be learned.

CHAPTER FOURTEEN

CREATING A RELATIONSHIP OF GRATITUDE

We nourish our relationship and participate in these exercises not only to enhance the potential stability of our marriage or partnership, but to create a fulfilling and comforting bond, one that can be a source of joy for both individuals devoting themselves to it. Living our life by honing in on what we are grateful for, as well as contemplating and expressing gratitude in our relationship is a foundation for warmth and connection that is infectious. Is our glass half full or half empty? Do we express our concerns about our partner more than our respect and admiration? In my own home, I often work late hours, and when I come home bursting through the door, my husband reaches for me with a big hug and says, "Thanks for coming home!" The first time he did this, I thought it was a little silly. Years later, I see and feel the wisdom in sharing gratitude for this small but powerful thought. It does require mindfulness to observe what is right and good in others to nurture and look for what is right even amidst what is wrong. Yes, mindfulness is needed to make a concerted effort to relate to the most pure and best parts of those near us. When we positively affirm our partner's strengths, the result is warmth, kindness, and affection in both directions. There are numerous health benefits. Train yourself to focus on gratitude since it is associated with positive mental health and emotional wellness. Learn to savor positive emotions longer because this has a transformative effect upon our relationship. Just as our tendency to replay negative and concerning events can cause us to magnify an angry and hurt mood, replaying joyful events or contemplating the positive characteristics of our partner accelerates our joy.

Conversely, it is truly a marvel the amount of missed opportunities and lack of gratitude that we will inadvertently expose our partners to. Many relationships create a culture of entitlement towards each other's time and attention, expressing demandingness without gratefulness. I am certain that many couples express more gratitude to waiters in trivial exchanges than they do to their partner on a regular basis. Think about it: we thank our waiter for a coffee refill, but we often have no idea what we could possibly thank our partner for. Remember, emotions form a complex web of interplay; we are always responding to each other's emotions.

Systems theory, which is a theoretical orientation that helps us to understand relationships, succinctly conceptualizes what happens in relationships. The theorists talk about feedback loops. This means that there is an exchange of information—a precipitating event and then a reaction to that event which then allows other events to unfold. When we make a critical statement to our partner, they may become irritated and respond in a further hurtful way, creating a negative feedback loop. We are also able to create positive feedback loops of joy and gratitude with each other. When we tell our partner how much we appreciate them or are thankful for something that they have done, they are more likely to respond favorably. We have unlimited capacity to expand each other's joys.

We feel deflated when we try our best to respond to our partners' needs or to do something special but our efforts are ignored or criticized. Feeling unappreciated and neglected is a factor that influences feeling of bitterness, hurt, and low engagement in the relationship. The human mind is often geared to take greater notice of events that are threatening or irritating, and then hold them, replaying them over and over again, all the while working ourselves into a greater fervor over our own irritation. We call this tendency rumination. We chew discontent over and over again like a meaty bone until our mouths are dripping with the bitter salivation of discontent. We do this to our partners too. We make *always* and *never* statements about each other, such as, *He always forgets to call,*' or, '*She never listens to me.*' Whether we are speaking these words or hearing them being doled out about us, we feel hurt, hopeless and even defensive. While the origin of our thoughts likely has some rational source, it is unlikely that words like always and never are truly accurate—nor is it ultimately the point. Our goal in speaking isn't to passively put down our partner, but to create change, hope and inspiration. This is achieved with optimism and gratitude.

A friend was recently sharing a story with me about her three year old son who is in preschool. He is going through a naked phase and he took off all of his clothes in front of the class. The teacher told the other children to look away and instructed him to please put his clothes back on. When I asked my friend what she planned to do about it, she said, "I plan to tell him, 'Thank you for putting your clothes back on when the teacher told you to.'" I really must clap and say bravo to such thoughtful parenting. We can all benefit from the mental gymnastics of finding what is good in a situation and expressing our gratitude for that. Have you ever missed the bus? How do you respond? Do you curse your poor luck or imagine that the rest of the day is doomed? What if you could sit down and say, "Wow, I am grateful for this extra 20 minutes until the next bus arrives; now I get to slow down."

As we develop our mindfulness meditation, the first thing that we seek to expel from our thoughts is our inner critic, the voice in our minds that tells us that we are not good enough, or that the situations we encounter are hopelessly negative. This is the voice that berates and punishes us in some sadistic attempt to make us better. When we allow ourselves to find motivation from this source, we end up exhausted and diminished. This inner critic finds expression in our outer words too, and when it is our primary way of relating to those around us, we exhaust and hurt more than cause understanding connection. It is very harmful and different from motivation sourced from a place of abundance and joy. Below are a few exercises to understand and achieve gratitude in love.

Exercise to develop an understanding the potency of language

First, close your eyes and find a comfortable seated position, whatever that means for you. Now you will find some words. I will recommend two, but you can use whatever is more relevant to you. You can do this with your partner or by yourself.

Say to yourself as a mantra, over and over again, the word 'hate.' Say it to yourself again, and again with your eyes closed and notice the kinds of thoughts which come to you. Notice the way that your body feels as the words tumble around in your mind. Just do it for about a minute or two. Notice your heart rate and the way your muscles feel when you repeat this.

Now do the same exercise, this time stating 'love.' Again, notice the contrast to the way that you feel when you meditate upon 'hate.' Most people state that their body feels more relaxed and open when they meditate upon love and gratitude instead of hate. In this way, we understand the significance of motivating others with gentleness and love, and not force and fury.

How to create more gratitude

Take the gratitude challenge in your relationship. Do it for a month. Each day, commit to finding two things that your partner says, does, or inspires in you, and state to your partner that you feel grateful for that. We really need to crank open our eyes a bit to heighten our awareness of how much there is to be grateful for. Some couples struggle with this since they imagine they won't have anything to say. When your partner comes home, you can use my favorite and say, "Thank you for coming home," or, "Thank you for answering the phone," "Thank you for sharing your smile," "Thank you for telling me about your day," etc. Our partner shouldn't need to write a sonnet or send three dozen flowers to receive a dollop of gratitude. When we are motivated to be grateful to each other, we seize the opportunity to find this everywhere. The more that we train ourselves to see it, the more that we will fill it. When we practice filling each other with gratefulness and seeing the best in each other, we will be more motivated. In turn, our relationship will be brimming with many positive feedback loops of joy and contentment.

CHAPTER FIFTEEN

COMPASSION AND EMPATHY

Compassion is a thing of true, raw beauty. It is an emotion that elevates us as humans beings to be able to feel what others feel, to imagine with our minds the experience of those around us and to care. Compassion is one of the cornerstones of mindfulness and Buddhism. When the Buddha saw the suffering of the world, he was inspired to help. Christ died for the sins of the world because he had compassion for them. We will not find any world religion that does not teach compassion. We will not find any healthy relationship without compassion. When we practice compassion, we cherish our partner's emotional experience and show it by centering our words and deeds around them. When we vow to love our partner, we promise to care about their feelings, to know them and to respond to them to the best of our ability. When we make decisions, we don't only think about how those choices affect us, but also how they will affect those around us.

Some personality types will naturally exhibit empathy very easily. Others require significant mindfulness and skill building to envisage their partner's emotions or to be able to evolve beyond the reflex of primal self needs. An empathetic relationship is one that is an emotional haven and offers safety and understanding that shelters us from the outside world. Imagine for instance that you have had a very terrible day, either at work or at home. Now if you are the type of person who likes to talk about what has happened, who do you want to share this bad day with? Is it your partner? Or, do you imagine that sharing it with your partner might make it worse? Generally, when others respond to our hurts and sadness with care and compassion, giving empathy and love, we naturally gravitate toward them. When our partner has a consistent pattern of being hostile, indifferent, or critical to us, we may begin to refrain from sharing. Imagine again that we told our partner that we were fired from work and they respond with, "Well, you didn't do a very good job; serves you right.' Even if we think that they went to work late and didn't do their tasks, this is not the time to respond with critical feedback. We must think about the hurt, sadness and grief that they are feeling and care first about their emotions. Remember, love is not about our own selfish needs being fulfilled; love is about the beloved other.

It is an interpersonal and cultural truth that most people start off their relationship being fairly empathetic with each other, but sometimes, particularly in struggling relationships, or when the partners are seeking therapy, they may revert to a completely self-centered attitude. Sometimes in the ailing relationship, we see couples who wouldn't speak to a raging stranger the way they address their partners—with cruelty, viciousness, and no conscious consideration of how their partner would feel. Typically, in the early stages of marriage counseling, when a therapist tries to reach into the lions' den and scoop up some of this venom to help the couple analyze it, each person dismisses this bad behavior by pointing to what they consider equally terrible treatment from the other person. It is because of a tendency to cling to our memories of anger, hurt and suffering that we falsely believe we are entitled to carry on in such a way. This is untrue. No matter what has happened in our relationship, we never gain the right to lose touch with our graciousness. We still are responsible for being empathetic, compassionate, and civil. Even if we are heading for the closest exit door, we owe it to ourselves to maintain our civility.

To create more compassion in your relationship, here are a few exercises that are known to help. Write a list of 50 things that you love about your partner. They can be things that are physical but mostly let them be things about their character and personality, for example, the way that they approach critical thinking and problem solving, or the kind of human being that they are. Last week, I made a social media post about how much I adore the way that my husband looks at a tree. When we are in love, we are obligated to create further inspiration for our love in even the most unlikely of places. Remember too, it's ok if it's difficult. We don't usually think in this way, so it will take some time and consideration.

Have you ever had a disagreement with your partner and when you notice that they are becoming upset, you get upset with them for being angry? The inner fallacy which says, *How dare you be angry!* needs to be expunged. What we really need to do is allow each other some internal space to feel, even making space for each other to experience the emotional spectrum of anger and sadness. Anger and Sadness, they too have their reasons and purpose for existing. We must strive to make it internally acceptable to experience the full spectrum of emotions because the *reaction* that we sometimes have to our emotions can and do become a problem. To regulate ourselves, we should use the skills discussed in previous chapters and take effort to pause. The next time you and your partner are each powering through a hard topic, take a breath. Then think about what emotions arose in your partner, whether it's anger, hurt, disappointment, whatever it may be. Try to respond to their emotion by openly labeling it (validation), "*I see you are feeling...*" hurt, frustrated, happy, apologetic, etc., or even a full blown, "*I am sorry that this is happening.*" Becoming aware of our partner's emotions and responding with empathy instead of defensiveness or attack indeed takes us very far.

Using compassion in the heat of a disagreement is an art that will dissipate many of our relational problems. If both partners can practice this sometimes, they will be well on their way to a strong relationship that stands the test of time.

CHAPTER SIXTEEN

PATIENCE

We could never learn to be brave or patient if there were only joy in the world.
—Helen Keller

Patience is a mindfulness and meditation jewel. When we practice our meditation and mindfulness, our reflective calm allows us to pause in between our breaths to really savor the experience of a long, slow deep exhalation. When we are patient, we are centered in the moment, *the now*. We create acceptance of the unknown and a curiosity about the present. Patience means that we wait with ease, without making waiting the master of our thoughts and deeds. Have you ever attempted a meditation and all you could think of the entire time was, "When will this be over? Oh, hurry up with breathing; hurry with the time. I am ready for the next big thing in my day." With that kind of narrow forward focus, we never really settle into the experience of the moment. With little patience, our relationships also take on a frantic quality. We are critical and judgmental, attempting to shape others with force by wielding the deft criticism of our words. Yet very few things evolve well when we approach them from this sharp and impatient angle, particularly our relationships with other people.

Patience with our partner means that we can be gentle with them and not force unnecessary expectations, nor project all our own values onto the way we imagine that they should be right now. When we practice this kind of calm acceptance, we encourage those around us to unfold at their own pace, in their own way, without imagining that we should all adhere to the same timeline. Patience further means that we can allow time and space to gather so that we can cool down from a heated disagreement and have space to rebalance ourselves. Patience gives space for reflection and belief that the right things will happen in the right time, which doesn't always need to be today or right now. Patience is the opposite of the calamity of demandingness; yet if we are in touch with our shadow self, we will acknowledge that demandingness is our ego self. Patience takes work! Demandingness is the ego's guise to push for what it wants in the moment without actual care for what other people need, want, or have capacity for in that moment. Perhaps it isn't all our fault, although Buddha would say that we are craving creatures full of desires that we imagine should be quelled. This human tendency is truly intensified by the design of modern culture. We have a whole culture built on instant messenger, instance results, instant feedback, fast food, fast track plans, etc. Our relationship will irritate us; our partner will irritate us. Even if we are 100% perfectly matched with our well-loved partner, they will sometimes get on our nerves. They will sometimes have different wants and needs and styles of doing things. All of this is perfectly ok. When our irritations arise, we get an opportunity to practice our aptitude for patience and care over ego.

What every couple should learn before taking their vows is that nothing will tax your capacity for patience as much as having a spouse and children. If we are ever to become effective and compassionate at maintaining these relationships, we must park our ego in the back seat and make space for others to show up with their needs. Our partner is twenty minutes late for dinner, patience. Our husband wants to take a different route to your favorite restaurant, patience. Your fourteen year old wants to start dressing in a new indie style, patience. Patience means that there is space between each person for there to be distinct differences and personalities without activating the impulse to turn everyone into a version of yourself. Patience means we let go of the impossible constraints that come from imagining that we can in fact control anything other than our own responses to life's circumstances. Becoming more patient in a radical world means that we have enhanced our ability to pause in between knowing and not knowing. We pause between thought and action, we take time to reflect on our feelings and consider the nature of our intended response before sharing it. Here is an elegant and simple way to expand our capacity for patience in the interaction with our partner.

Yes, you will need paper: It is only by becoming very familiar with yourself and what makes you feel impatient that you can cultivate greater patience. First make a long, long list of the things that cause you irritation. You may want to keep a piece of paper or electronic note with you through the week so that you can make a record of each time you feel irritated or impatient. Take it seriously and get real with yourself. If you reacted, you should also make a note of that. The purpose of this exercise will be to expand our ability to pause before reacting. So when you're talking, going, thinking, moving, discussing and debating, in between your thought and response, create a pause. There is an entire universe of alternate opportunities within a pause between our impulse and action. We should always try to insert a long breath there. We have a boundless potential within mindfulness based stress reduction and body awareness which can diffuse many disagreements. We create a more centered and compassionately wise version of ourselves with our breathing, so let us go through some examples of how we use this. Your husband bursts into the room while you're in the middle of a phone call and wants to chat about his golf score. Before reacting with shooing him away, take a deep breath and reflect on how grateful you are that he wants to share his life with you before signaling that you need a minute. Your wife is having an argument with your daughter about the color of bows that she wants to wear in her hair. Your reaction is to jump in and snap "I told you to let her choose for herself!" Pause, breathe, think about how much both you and your partner want what's best for your child before responding. It is in the moment of breathing in a cleansing energy and enjoying its calming effect that our mind's eye sees the best parts of our partner. Our response will then be filled with faithful optimism, kindness and acceptance.

The second exercise to help with this is to keep a journal for two weeks. Each time you notice yourself feeling impatient, write down a bit more about it. What are your triggers for feeling impatient? By knowing them very intimately, we are able to best forge a constructive response to our needs and those of our partner.

CHAPTER SEVENTEEN

CREATING AN EMOTIONALLY SUPPORTIVE MARRIAGE

When developing our own mindfulness or meditation practice, one of the skills that we work to enhance is that of labeling and analyzing our emotions. We notice our emotions and attempt to delay reacting to them or judging them with criticism. It is challenging to achieve the gentle acceptance of our feelings. Our whole culture is one which esteems the scientific outcome but casts aside the human emotions that inspired the quest in us to strive toward for achievement in the first place. We are at an even greater deficit when it comes to the topic of accepting and responding to emotions such as anger, hurt, sadness, and guilt. We simply do not know how to be open enough to create the time and space to deliver responses that offer compassion, comfort, and acceptance of the feelings for ourselves and others. As we learn the skill of moving towards our partner's emotions, we deepen our bonds and enhance our understanding of each other. There is a vast wisdom within the emotional. Ultimately, this is one of the greatest ways to make our connection with our partner sacred and empathetically connected.

One of the barriers to developing an emotionally accepting, feeling-charged, love bond is the phenomenon I call, "Tell me what you're feeling and I will tell you how to fix it." This happens when we listen to each other with positive intentions, but instead of providing an opportunity to process emotions and participate in the act of sharing thoughts and feelings, we quickly respond to our partners' concerns with the 'solution' to their problems. Unfortunately, our partner who is sharing their emotions doesn't get the calming benefit of more deeply processing their feelings. Furthermore, we can add more to their tension or end up hurting our partner by our well-meaning feedback. Let us put it in a different way: when someone comes to us with a problem, they usually don't want us to fix the problem, they just want to be heard.

Imagine our partner is complaining about a difficult colleague, and the most recent horrible thing that Jane from the office has done includes taking the paper-clips from your wife's desk and gossiping about her to a mutual colleague. Suppose that our partner has already tried some solutions, everything from not engaging with Jane, to tuning out her snarky comments, to even feigning friendship. If we listen and say, "You need to do something about this; you can't keep living like this every day. You need to report her to HR again," we risk causing our love to feel belittled, controlled, or that their own problem solving is inferior. Here our partner is turning to us to vent their feelings, but instead of understanding, they receive a laundry list of things they didn't do right. It is most often the male gender who uses problem solving when their partners come to them with an issue. For better or worse, men want to help, but for women, the solution is listening with empathy. The truth is that most of the time, when we share a bad day at work or at home, when we share something traumatic that happened to us in our childhood or past, when we talk about what happened with the kids, we want to enjoy the feeling of being heard and understood. A response of "That sounds like a really tough day," is really what makes a person feel understood. If you still have the perfect solution hanging onto the lips of your mouth, then before offering it, ask first! The phrase, "Can I offer you a bit of advice on this?" will go a far way with your partner.

Providing attention is the first and most important step in all of these mindfulness exercises. We can call it attention or focused awareness, but they both mean exactly the same thing: tuning in and staying there. We put down our phone and look at the other person without turning away our gaze for any reason. Here we lavish presence on each other. Even if you do only one thing to start working toward an emotionally charged and supportive relationship, let it be this. When we know that our spouse cares enough to turn their eyes away from the phone, television or computer in order to listen when we walk into the room ranting about some challenge from the day, we settle down just a little bit more knowing that they care enough to make hearing us a priority.

The opposite of this is when our partner ignores our attempts to talk to them. Emotional neglect cuts like a knife and causes relationships to feel very hollow and lonely before the marriage sputters to a complete failure. Some of us purposefully tune out because we are terrified of not saying the right thing, terrified of connecting on such a deep level or perhaps before reading this book, ignorant of the significance of providing attention. Of course, we know that we are not always going to get it right every time, and our partner doesn't expect us to either. Sometimes when they buzz into the room with a flurry of feeling, we may be in the middle of a work email or not be feeling well and we will miss their cue completely. The positive side to this is that when we have a good track record with our partner, they will remember that we do have good intentions. This time we didn't connect completely, and that makes prioritizing responsiveness even more important when the next occasion turns up.

How to mindfully care and support means that we anchor ourselves in, and consistently and purposefully observe and respond to the emotional experience of our partner through a focused and relentless lens of compassion for them. We seek to understand the emotions behind their dialogue and to be with them in the expression of their emotional spectrum. We will do an exercise which will help with expanding our ability to do this.

Following up with consistency is a two-way interpersonal mechanism. It means that we form a pattern in our relationship of providing attention focused on soliciting emotion and also following up on what has been said on previous occasions. Maybe a day or two after talking with our partner about something that happened to them, we check in again and ask, *How are you feeling about* _____ *now?* We show that we listen and remember what is being shared.

Heart Meditation: Try the following exercise meant to intercept the potential for going into 'fixer mode,' as well as to enhance our focus on emotions. The next time that your partner comes to you with something that has happened to them, know that this is your opportunity to practice this skill.

1) Focus, put down the phone, and turn away from whatever else is going on. It will still be there in ten minutes after this conversation is over.

2) Practice heart listening. This means look at the expressions on their face, tune into the speech. Is it fast? Slow? Are their cheeks red with emotion? Are their brows furrowed? Really hear them. Imagine a cord, a tightly woven cord that is attached to both of you. Let their emotion come into you. Be sure that you are practicing active listening, which means you keep your body turned toward them. Allow your arms to be open and let everything about your posture and focus indicate: *I am here with you.* Then, as you continue to hear, forming a picture of the feeling that they are experiencing, imagine that feeling penetrating through the cord and into you. You say, "How hurtful/frustrating/wonderful, _____." State the emotion and feel it together. Remember don't follow up with solutions or an alternate way of doing things unless they make a specific request for advice. Try it even though it may feel artificial. The more difficult this exercise, the more this tells us that we will benefit from practicing heart meditation and expanding our awareness of our feeling states.

CHAPTER EIGHTEEN

CELEBRATING JOYS

Couples have often imagined that relationship satisfaction is mostly influenced by having conflict management solutions and enhancing their friendship in such a way that prevents them from developing too many heated battles. While yes, it is true that conflict management and resolution does influence happiness in love, there are other relationship skills which do outrank whittling down conflict. For the couples that I have helped over the years, one very consistent predictor of satisfaction in marriage is related to how much couples celebrate their joys together. We are naturally drawn to sharing information about our daily lives, successes and inner dialogue with those who share enthusiasm about what contributes to our joy.

Consider the last time something really exciting happened to you. Maybe the promotion came through, you received great news about your health, you heard from someone you had been missing, or something happened that really made your day. You turned to your partner to talk about it. How did they respond? How did you feel about the way that they responded? Did you feel supported, understood and connected? Did it feel that they were genuinely excited for you? I know recently I was asked to be a guest on a television show as an expert on marriage counseling. My husband tuned in and when

I got home, he gave me the biggest hug and kiss. He exalted, "You were amazing and so professional; I am so proud of you!" He had even grilled us a delicious celebratory dinner. It made for a wonderful evening and it was wonderful to connect with my husband over that professional victory. Let us examine the mechanisms of joy and then form a plan for how we can create some opportunities to enhance the joy in your relationship. We can also discuss in greater detail some of the barriers to expanding joy before finishing with a mindfulness exercise to expand our relationship happiness.

We can hold tight to our bliss. Clinically, psychology helps us understand that we can intensify our irritations, anxieties, and sadness by ruminating, the tendency of our anxious and melancholy minds to put our sorrow or potential failings on replay, basically chewing on them in our thoughts. Rumination aggravates emotional disease and accelerates pain. The mind does have the ability to feel emotions repeated for our own viewing. When we become mindful of rumination, we can choose something different for our viewing pleasure. We can also expand our hearts' contentment by being purposeful in what we think about and how we think about it. We can relish our happiness as well as the happiness of our spouse or partner.

When we tune into our partners' emotions and provide empathy for them, positive emotions as well as anger and hurt, we gain a world of wisdom as we also strengthen our marital bond. The manner in which we respond to each other does create a magical interplay where we are co-creating emotional, hormonal, and biochemical exchanges that yield physical and emotional resonance, the magnetic pull between us. It can be undeniably wonderful or it can repel us from each other. When our partner enters the room with a look of happiness on their face, do we mirror that, do we light up too, asking with wonder, "What is your lovely smile about?" Can we allow ourselves to listen and smile and laugh together, sharing in the glee of the life that we share together?

If you answer no, you are being honest in your observation that you and/or your partner do not slow down and share your joys with each other. There are different categories of reasons for this.

Emotional avoidance means that we are averse to tuning into emotions, due to fear or ignorance. We blunt heightened emotion and avoid being too excited or talking about what has hurt us. Sometimes this happens because we have received too many signals in childhood or beyond that feelings are dangerous. Maybe our parents scolded us for crying as children or that some other emotionally shaming lesson has constricted our outward expression of feeling. Another reason for preventing us from celebrating joy with our partner is the epidemic of inattention. We turn to our work, our phones, the news, and countless other diversions. At the same time, real people around us are starving for connection, hungering for celebration while sitting next to us feeling alone, but we don't notice as we chat with someone hundreds of miles away with the marvel of instant messenger. Obviously, a balance is necessary. We cannot give our attention all of the time but we must give it completely some of the time, and during those times when we are giving our attention, it should be utterly undivided for at least some portion of the day. If your response is, how can I make time to do this when between the kids and work I barely have time to brush my teeth? Well then you shouldn't fool yourself into thinking that you want a relationship.

One other relationship factor which inhibits our ability to celebrate joy is depression, or melancholy. Without treatment, a person suffering from depression will not be able to celebrate or see their own happiness—least of all somebody else's. In fact, depression works in two ways, by the presence of negative emotions as well as the absence of positive emotions. If it is more than the blues or a little slump and instead is full blown depression, treatment may be necessary before the symptoms can abate. If your partner is truly depressed, you may feel very alone and frustrated in your inability to reach them. If this is a long-standing condition, it is likely that you have had to internalize the hurt and distance. You may have become a social architect, rediscovering other people who you can rely upon for emotional connection, but this is no consolation for the sadness and frustration over not being able to celebrate and connect with your chosen life partner.

The final reason for failing to celebrate each other's joys is the less common tendency towards competition or jealousy in the relationship. Jealousy is a human emotion and can have positive effects, but if our partner is frustrated and humiliated over their own recent loss of job, and we have just landed the promotion of our dreams, they might not be emotionally equipped to be happy for us in the way that we would like them to. Other relationships are consistently starved for celebration of each other. It is an unfortunate fact that women who are professionally successful sometimes are more likely to be ignored for their achievements or even put down by their partners. This is especially true if they hold degrees that are higher than their partners' or have a higher earning capacity. While there are many male/female dyadic relationships where both partners nurture and celebrate each other equally, this is not always the case. Culture and gender roles dictate that women are expected to be bombastic cheerleaders of others. This acculturation means that endlessly cheering a partner, even from the side lines, comes more easily for women from childhood on. Men who find it more natural to encourage their partners' success usually have a high degree of emotional awareness and have often been deeply nurtured as children.

Attunement and mirroring: Mirroring is a way of behaving that is often talked about in behavioral psychology. It means that we tune in to each other's non-verbal and verbal behavior and synchronize with them. There is evidence saying that we respond favorably to those by whom we are mirrored. Any sales associate who studies their craft, including waitresses, purposefully mirror their customers outperform their competitors. Just imagine, you are seated at your favorite restaurant and the server comes by asking for your order. You smile and shrug your shoulders, "Well, guess I will have the lobster bisque and crab cakes!" She also smiles and shrugs her shoulders, "Why not?!" You are likely not aware of how or why, but you feel comfortable with her and like her. You will unconsciously remember that when you are writing her tip at the end of the dinner.

In examining parent-child relationships, mirroring is a strong predictor of what kind of relationship will develop between a mother and infant. For mothers who mirror the gaze of their children, who feel sadness with their babies and feel excitement and wonder with their newborns, they ultimately create secure attachment bonds. The literature is full of evidence for the benefits all through life for adults who had secure attachments to their parents in childhood. In mother child relationships where the mothers keep a neutral face or do not lock on to the child's facial expressions, the relationship becomes what is referred to clinically as 'insecure/dismissing attachments.' This means that infants are less likely to look at their mothers or turn to them for soothing when in distress. We learn much about relationships from this. It is exactly what we have been talking about in this book—we must learn to and practice tuning into each other's emotions for the intimate connection within our relationships to thrive.

Here is an exercise of attunement that you can do without your partner even knowing it. We don't need all of our exercises to be practiced very formally. The whole purpose of doing an exercise is to increase the likelihood that you will incorporate these lessons in a way that they become a natural part of the relationship. When we are doing our best, we are practicing mindful awareness of our partner or spouses' emotional state. Do this every day for a week. Notice what they are feeling at the end of the day. Ask more questions. Ask, "What was the highpoint of your day?" You can do this even if you spent the entire day together. Notice the way their facial expressions may change as they discuss something that was very joyful or exciting about their day. Hold their gaze, notice the nuances of the expressions that they make when they are enthusiastic. Maybe their eye brows go upwards and their face tightens a bit, elevating their entire expression. Perhaps they smile in recounting what was good about their day. This is where you mirror: imagine all of their positive energies pouring out from them and you can scoop those positive feelings up and send them right back, creating a buzz of joyful excitement between you. Be mindful of holding their gaze and of keeping the same expressions they do, validating and nodding. Tell them, "You look so happy." or "I can see your excitement when you talk about this." Or "I love sharing this happiness with you!" or all of the above statements. Remember, when we mirror each other we use both our non-verbal expressions like facial cues and body language, as well as the verbal cues like the tone and choice of words. Pay attention to how they respond with your mindful attention focused on their joys.

CHAPTER NINETEEN

INTIMACY

Intimacy is the culmination or the true melting pot of all of the rest of the relationship. It is the feeling of being understood and known by our partner; it is the indescribable essence of being firmly and warmly connected to our beloved. An intimate relationship is one where there are all forms of love and bonding present: emotional, spiritual, and physical. The act of experiencing sensual connection is a beautiful one. The thirst for lust and orgasm is a primal desire out of which humanity has been born. There is a natural flux to sexual energy. Through the lifespan, through our emotional and relational tumults, our sexual desire may ebb and flow. All of this is normal.

Sex usually happens fluidly and naturally between two partners when all of the other pieces of their relationship are in order, without having to talk too much about it. At other times, in order to sustain intimacy, we must be capable of having honest communication with each other about exactly what is happening when something does not feel right or when the sexual frequency has changed. Many people who come in for couples counseling become very uncomfortable when they try to even say the word sex. We cannot blame ourselves for this. Many parents follow our culture, which is ridden with conflict about sexuality. Culturally we favor lessons on the prohibition of sexuality and the encouragement of no sex before matrimony, instead of honoring what it means to be sexually empowered and intimately healthy. Bring your awareness to yourself and before you attempt to gauge anything else, first think about how comfortable you are to discuss sex. Can you talk with your partner with ease or do you blush and stutter or just avoid the topic completely. Without a vocabulary and some degree of comfort in discussing sex, it is likely that we are suffering from sexual shame and this could bleed into our sexual behavior with our spouse. As adults, we should focus on being able to tell our partner what our sexual preferences are, what makes us feel good as well as what things we prefer to avoid in the bedroom and beyond. It is also quite ok to use non-verbals in the heat of the moment or some blend of verbal and non-verbal communication to share our pleasures in a sexual moment. We should also be able to ask our partner what they enjoy in terms of physical touch. Ironically, we also must be free to say no to sex if we are going to enjoy sex with our spouse. However, if we feel obligated to give in to our partners' sexual needs because they use guilt or fear tactics when we try to decline, then we are doing little more than practicing sexual servitude, which doesn't often lead to much pleasure. At the same time, it is true that there may be certain occasions when we agree to have sex because we care about our partner's needs, and at those occasions, we might even find it enjoyable after we start the process. This is normal as long as we maintain that we are able to decline if we choose.

When we enter a discussion about intimacy, most people immediately summon thoughts of sex and sexual touch. While those are significant and important parts of intimate connection, intimacy is so much more than this. In fact it is very easily true that two people can have sex without sharing any intimacy at all. Our hook up culture can attest to this reality. Many relationships go through periods of low sexual frequency but they can still enjoy the benefits of sustaining deep and rich intimacy. Physical touch can be divided into two distinct forms, sexual and non-sexual touch. Sexual touch is easy to understand. It is the exchange of physical affections which precedes or takes place during sex itself. Non-sexual touching is the vast territory of everything else. It is the hand we hold, a gentle caress of our partner's cheek or arm while standing in line at the grocery store. It is reaching and pausing to savor a hug after a long day or work. All of the physical connection that happens outside of the bedroom is the fabric and the glue of the sexual intimacy which happens in the bedroom. Relationships which enjoy a high degree of non-sexual touch generally feel securely anchored and closely connected. For some partners, sexual intimacy and touch are a more vital component of the relationship than for others. Many things can stand in the way of building this kind of intimacy, such as a history of trauma or sexual dysfunction, fear of intimacy or frequent conflicts. Due to these reasons or from sheer neglect, it may become difficult to sustain both sexual or non-sexual touch, even if the relationship started with plenty of it.

One barrier which prevents sexual intimacy and is a consistent presence in our lives is variations in sleep schedules. It is intuitive that we would have more opportunities for intimate, sexual and non-sexual encounters if we go to bed at the same time. Research does support this notion, so if we want to increase the likelihood of having time to be close with each other, it is wise to follow along when your partner says that they are winding down at night. Even the act of cuddling can enrich the bond we have with our partner. Having a ritual for how we go to sleep such as hugging and kissing good night does keep the connection strong.

One of the questions that I often ask couples who come to me for marriage counseling is, "Why do you have sex with each other?" Often I see two people pause here to reflect upon a question that they had never asked themselves before. So, when you stop and think about it, what do you come up with? Is it something you do like you do the laundry or going to work every day? A task you manage because you feel obligated? Is it something that both you and your partner enjoy and look forward to? Are both you and your partner able to enjoy sex and are you able to reach orgasm? A healthy sexual relationship can consist of many variations of pleasure and passion. Becoming mindful of our sexual union with our spouse means that there is a sense of pleasure and desire which both gives and receives freely. It means that we allow physical intimacy to be a time when we create a connection of sensual pleasure, sharing of our bodies and expressing our love in the most personal way. We must be truly comfortable with ourselves and our flesh to be able to enjoy our sexual relationship. In fact, feeling uncomfortable with our physical bodies is another reason that people sometimes begin to avoid sex.

Couples sometimes struggle with the sacred acts of Giving and Receiving. For example, there can be an imbalance in a relationship where one person initiates sex most of the time. It is a sign of sexual dysfunction if only one person is making attempts to foster sexual connection and the other is left to only say yes or no in that moment. The person who is doing the initiating often craves feeling desired and is longing for mutual intimacy. Furthermore, in terms of giving and receiving after the process of sexual intimacy has begun, there is a continued need to evaluate both partners' ability to give and receive in the acts of foreplay and penetrative sex. Does each person both value and prioritize allowing time and space to reach heightened sexual arousal? In male/female pairs, it is one of nature's great mysteries that women take significantly longer to reach full sexual arousal, several minutes in fact, while men can reach peak sexual arousal in under a minute. For the act of sex to be pleasurable, both persons much be in full arousal. Practicing mindfulness of each other's differing biological needs is imperative to reach the balance of mutual sexual satisfaction. While the mindset in approaching sex should be one of presence and stillness in the moment, many individuals and couples go off target here and they approach the act of sex as one would approach mutual masturbation. They are aware only of the end goal of the sexual act, which in their mind is to achieve orgasm. So much is lost when we don't become aware of the other depths of sexual union. It is true that I have known paraplegics who had healthy sexual lives with their partners—which is because they know the great secrets of the potential beauty of intimacy. To enjoy sex together, we don't even need to have a phallus or an operable vaginal cavity. We don't have to be able to ejaculate or have an erection—sex is so much more than that.

A massage can be an act of intimate pleasure when the aim is to slow down, tune out everything else and focus on feeling and celebrating each other's physical pleasure.

Some barriers to entering this deeper level of sexual expression exist in our fear state. Some of us contend with so much internal chatter that it is impossible to really be present with ourselves and least of all to even be aware of our own real needs. Sometimes we enter the sexual arena wanting to gain the accolades and bravado of a performance well done. We focus so much on getting it right or following a script that we completely fail to be present with our partner in the sexual journey. In other instances, we focus too much attention on the goal of orgasm and so we rush into making it our main accomplishment, but the whole time the sensual experience feels artificial and hurried. This is the opposite of mindful sex. To build intimacy, we should at times have sex that does not penetrate, that uses many other forms of sexual pleasure such as oral and manual. Both the variety and spontaneity of allowing other forms of pleasure to come into our bedroom will enhance the delight of both persons.

Mindful Sex exercise: The goal of sex is connection, time spent touching, smelling, tasting and being with each other's flesh. In this exercise, we will focus on a full submersion, a total sensory and mindful sex experience. The purpose is to become present with our partner and focusing on each outlet for taking them into us.

Visually, first we see our partner. We look into their eyes and we see the rest of them through the lens of love and vulnerability. We spend a few moments really being here with this vision.

We smell them. In fact there is a lot of information about the role that the olfactory senses play in sexual desire. What we call attraction is actually the result of the exchange of hormones that we smell in each other, which signals to our DNA that this person will be a favorable sexual match for reproduction. Yet we have sex for many reasons beyond conceiving a child together. We come close to our partner's face and every other part of their body and we inhale them, bringing our awareness to the uniqueness of their scent as we kiss them. We really bring our awareness to this act of smelling and take pleasure in our body's ability to bring intoxicating scent inside us.

We taste. We must be very open to all avenues for sexual pleasure to be able to love, to taste their mouth and their body with love and desire. Just as infants use their mouths to understand the world, we as adults use our mouths, our lips and our tongues, to bring sensual pleasure to our spouse. Savoring the taste of their flesh and noticing what their tongues and bodies feel like in our mouth.

We touch. This means that we explore our partner's body with our hands. We can use our fingertips as well as our whole hands. We don't just dive into the erotic zones to fulfill touch—we touch them everywhere from head to toe, and everywhere in between that they feel comfortable being touched. We touch the erotic zones last, particularly for women, manual stimulation of the vagina is much more pleasurable after they are at least partially aroused.

Finally, we listen. We want to hear their sounds of sexual pleasure and their breathing which indicates sexual arousal and climax. Simultaneously we must be willing and able to have those conversations about what went well in the sex and to even boldly ask if there is anything that they didn't enjoy. We should seek to tune in with our whole selves in mindful sex. When all of our senses are tuned into the other, we are in a state of meditation and communion with them. This is a deep experience of spirituality and being human.

This is mindfulness in sex. This is what it means to be present and aware and really with our partners in an act of loving pleasure. If you notice in the above exercise, there is no talk of sexual penetration. If you as a couple do not incorporate penetrative sex into the exercise, it takes away nothing from the act of connection and pleasure that can be experienced together with mutual mindfulness and presence.

The achievement of a mindful sexual and intimate relationship with one's spouse is the crown jewel of a marriage which has prioritized commitment, communication, and has a deep trusting emotional connection. Yet it is worth every bit of work that it takes to achieve.

Following this prescription is a path to nowhere. We are not aiming to reach orgiastic delight but instead we nuzzle comfortably into our partner. Perhaps in no other avenue is the path to mindfulness more submissive than in the act of being sensual and enjoying eroticism with our partner. While there are many types of erotic moments that you will enjoy in your relationship, from the proverbial *quicky*, to the slow, languorous afternoon, when the mind is unfettered and the day is long, there is beauty in enjoying this kind of love making.

CHAPTER TWENTY

MINDFULLY CONNECTING THROUGH TIME

Making our relationships sacred by instilling it with time intentionally meant to bond and to reconnect, we must create opportunities to check in and manage any aspect of life together. Some aspects should be understood more deeply, like parenting, sharing household duties, and work life. Some of our time together should be playful, relaxed and non-goal oriented. We should have things that we look forward to doing each day as a part of the time that we spend with our partner. Do you have time like that in your relationship, moments when you cherish being together, listening, reading, talking, cooking? While it is important that each couple creates and shares its own version of time for connection, we can also study this compiled list of some of the more common mindful moments that happy couples who I have worked with have used successfully. Mindful moments are times that each person has set aside to focus on being together and bonding. Some of that time can just as well be spent along with the kids, family, and friends, and for other mindful moments you and your spouse can be by yourselves too. You must not be alone.

When we create our list of aspirational mindful relationship moments, we must give these times top priority in our schedule with some degree of consistency. If we haven't done that in the past, our partner may find it doubtful that we can do it in the present. It is important to bring optimism and enthusiasm into the equation to achieve maximum gain when carving out this time to be together. Thinking of a few that work for both of you already, what times do you spend in the relationship or family that you look forward to regularly?

Waking up can be a really special time, and some couples make that a mindful moment by bringing each other coffee or tea in bed. It is something that takes ten minutes but that really sets the tone for the rest of the day.

For other daily rituals, many couples love cooking together. Since we already are going to eat something, doing it together can be a fantastic way to collaborate. The collaboration can also take place during the day as you discuss what you would like to prepare and the shopping that can go into it.

Dining together. Many happy couples devote their meal time or dinner to putting away their phones and sharing their meal. If you are parents, this often means the children are dining together too, which could have positive impacts upon the health and academic benefits for kids. As a couple, this means that you may use this time to talk about your day, asking what was the best part of your day, what was the most difficult part of your day. If the dinner table is a cell phone and television free zone, then you are more than likely to enjoy bonding during the meal.

A mindful marriage may make time together to go for a walk or take the pets for a walk.

Sharing in fitness is something that a couple can bond with. So is time spent outdoors enjoying the benefits of nature's sounds together along with the physical benefits of exercise.

Gardening together is a collaborative activity and a metaphor for what we do with planting the seeds of our relationship. It also makes time to be together and harvest the result of your efforts. There are many health benefits to gardening and touching the healing soil of the earth with the bare flesh of our hands.

Sleeping ritual. As we covered in previous sections, going to sleep together helps make time for bonding and being together. This is also time that you can use to discuss the following day or process things that happened during the day. A good question that some couples ask each other as they prepare for slumber is, "What do you hope that you dream about tonight?"

Checking in throughout the day. If you're like most couples, you are not able to spend your entire day together. Exchanging a text or two, or even a phone call during the day works well for some couples.

Make your intention to come together and come apart mindful by hugging, kissing, and saying "I love you." Coming together and coming apart can become a mindful moment.

On a weekly basis, a couple can create rituals around managing the business of sharing their lives and household duties. For instance, budgeting and writing out the bills together is a helpful way for some to manage the necessity of all of the tedious things that must be done.

Do a weekly check in. In my practice with couples, I call this the 'emotional clearinghouse.' This is time that you set aside to have conversations about things that have come up between you. Lead with positivity and share what your partner has done that week that felt right and made you feel connected and supported. You can also use this time to discuss something that you would like to work towards, a relationship goal. This could be a gentle way of reframing something that disappointed you in the previous week. Instead of sharing it as a criticism, you reframe it as a need.

Plan housing projects like cleaning, remodels, redecorating together, and even if these things are of little interest to one of you, be mindful to nurture the things that are important to your partner.

Take a class, a workshop, or learn a new hobby together. Perhaps each of you could write a list of items that you would like to do, then take turns actually doing them. Dancing, cooking, pottery, hiking, mountain climbing. By sharing active interest in planning these activities together, the relationship is revived.

If you have children, share in enjoying family life together, instead of passing the kids off to each other and doing separate activities. Be sure that you are at least spending time together as a group weekly.

Find other groups on meetup and make friends together. Having friends is vital for the relationship. We all must have others who we turn to bring excitement and comradery into our life. There is a reason that marriages often take place in front of witnesses. We need the support of our community to stay on track with our relationship goals and commitment to life together. There are groups that are focused on fun, such as playing games or eating at local brunch restaurants, as well as therapeutic psychoeducational groups that focus on talking about the relationship.

Take a vacation together. Listen to each person's ideal vacation and then decide which would be best to do together. Remember, planning the trip is just as exciting as experiencing it, and then reliving the memories together afterwards.

CONCLUSION

Creating a relationship mindfully is a skill, but very few people will start off in a marriage or relationship exhibiting this skill naturally. We learn by trial and error. Sometimes we become our best selves after making mistakes for years. We began our relationship to give and receive love. Maintaining that same hopeful and rich bond takes years of practice, work and sometimes grieving through years of hurt and disappointment leftover from when we were not getting it right.

The first step to understanding is to learn more about ourselves, to open our minds and pasts to introspection. When we learn more about ourselves and how we relate to all others, we can then form an intimate understanding of how to learn more about our partner to create a relationship that nourishes each unique partner.

A healthy relationship is one in which both persons are free to feel and healthily express the breadth and width of emotions and behaviors, and in which both people are able to respond to the emotional and intellectual expressions of their partners most of the time, with support and care. A mindful relationship is one in which we attempt to understand and soothe each other's hurts of yesterday and today, and to celebrate the enthusiasms of the small and large moments.

A mindful relationship is one where we forgive. Each fresh day is a new chance to improve our connection with our love. Whether emotional, physical, or communicative, each component serves as a separate vital pathway to enhance our bond. When the energy is blocked in any one of these areas, other parts of them can ail and hurt, leading to disease in the relationship. A nurturing and warm love sustains our hope and health. It echoes into the hearts of those around us and vitalizes every part of our life.

By observing with non-judgement and active awareness which parts of our relationship may be in need of strengthening, we also become aware of the path to fixing it. With the hopefulness of these pages, we can learn the mechanisms of mindfulness and learn how to become more deeply connected.

It takes courage to have hope and belief in a relationship and to let go of hurt and anger, instead replacing it with positivity and healing. But, we must shed the leaves to grow the buds and flowers of light and love. All of it is worth the work—love, connection, care, empathy and the celebration of everything that it means to be a human being.

BIBLIOGRAPHY

Barnes, S., Brown, K. W., Krusemark, E., Campbell, W. K., & Rogge, R. D. The role of mindfulness in romantic relationship satisfaction and responses to relationship stress. *J Marital Fam Ther*. 2007 Oct;33(4): 482–500. doi: 10.1111/j.1752-0606.2007.00033.x. PMID: 17935531

Gunn, H. E., Buysse, D. J., Hasler, B. P., Begley, A., & Troxel, W. M. "Sleep Concordance in Couples is Associated with Relationship Characteristics," *Sleep* 38, no. 6 (2015):933–939. http://doi.org/10.5665/sleep.4744

Larson, N., MacLehose, R., Fulkerson, J. A., Berge, J. M., Story, M., & Neumark-Sztainer, D. "Eating Breakfast and Dinner Together as a Family: Associations with Sociodemographic Characteristics and Implications for Diet Quality and Weight Status," *Journal of the Academy of Nutrition and Dietetics* 113, no. 12 (2013):1601–1609. http://doi.org/10.1016/j.jand.2013.08.011

Miller, D. P., Waldfogel, J., & Han, W. J. (2012). Family meals and child academic and behavioral outcomes. *Child development*, 83(6), 2104–2120. https://doi.org/10.1111/j.1467-8624.2012.01825.x Accessed January 26th 2018.